The Warrior

and

the Little Girl

Discover your Duality.
Create power and joy in your work life.

by
Geri Rhoades

Tanzanite Press, Massachusetts

Printed in the United States of America
First Printing: April 2005
Tanzanite Press, Massachusetts
Orders at Tanzanitepress.com

Cover art: Theresa Seelye.
Cover design: Chuck Seelye.

Rhoades, Geri
The Warrior and The Little Girl/ Geri Rhoades
Library of Congress Control Number: 2005903324
    1. Business   2. Self-Help   3. Women's Issues

ISBN 0-9767813-0-1

Author's note: The names and details of the examples provided in this book have been changed to respect the confidentiality of the participant. The author and publisher specifically disclaim any liability that is incurred from the use or application of the contents of this book.

Visit the Renewed Direction website at:
www.reneweddirection.com

To my son Stephen.
You are my inspiration
in helping to make the world a better place.

And to my brother Joe who is no longer with us.
He admired my Warrior since I was a Little Girl.

Acknowledgments

Writing this section feels like it must feel to those who get up to accept an Academy Award. I am grateful to many and know I will forget someone.

First, thank you to my two fabulous editors, Abby Bass and Dawn Simmons. Your attention to detail and belief in my work ensured the integrity of the final product. I could not have done this without you.

Thank you to my grandmother Annie, my first example of a Warrior and Little Girl. You are gone, but not forgotten. To her daughter, my mother, who taught me how to "own the room." And, to my sister Eva, who owns the room better than anyone.

Thank you to the over 75 women who participated in the study. I promised you confidentiality so I can't name you. You know who you are and I appreciate your contribution and honesty.

A special thanks to all the people, men and women, I have worked with over the years. These experiences helped me formulate my work and whether positive or challenging, I learned a great deal.

And finally, to my life-partner Malcolm. Your unending support and encouragement is priceless.

Contents

As I walk along the shadows of the memories in my mind
I see visions of my yesteryears and the peace I couldn't find
I see dreams and broken promises from the loves I've left behind
And the visions seem so clear to me and the memories not too kind

And the peace I couldn't find would taunt me through the years
Like a treat beyond my reach, like the hope beyond my tears
And the peace I couldn't find was the very thing I feared
For the day I stopped to look inside the shadows disappeared

And it was bright and it was beautiful and as simple as a mime
For the peace I recently found was right here all the time.

Introduction

An incredible number of women have been leaving the traditional workplace for something new or nothing altogether. In fact, women are leaving at twice the rate of men, and women-owned businesses are growing at twice the rate of the national average. Many are disenchanted, unsatisfied and unfulfilled with what they thought would be empowering and satisfying.

For years they have read books on playing like a man, playing the game, getting the corner office and getting to the top. Most haven't made it there. In fact, not everyone wants the top, yet where they are isn't rewarding either. These books approach success as a list of things to do, or not do, but not as a way of being. If success and fulfillment were a checklist, we would all be where we want to be and happy to be there.

We've gotten a lot of advice we try to follow, about all the things we shouldn't do as women, and how we should be more like men. What's missing is the acceptance that we are women who think differently, act differently, are motivated differently and can't be the same as men and feel good in our own skin. What's missing is the acknowledgement that "girl" is not a bad four letter word. What's missing is the acknowledgement that there is a very powerful possibility for women to successfully combine the great attributes of being a girl, manage the stereotypical challenges with traits that are untapped and combine the masculine and feminine; adding tremendously to the corporate environment. There is a unique opportunity to explore, cultivate and showcase this possibility, to bring us both power and joy.

Over the years I've had great success in my career, and I've run into trouble. I was either Wonder Woman (co-workers would come to me to get a job done), Wonderless Woman (my work would be attacked), too threatening (co-workers and subordinates would be afraid of me and tell me I was intimidating) or too appealing (co-workers would comment on my friendly and optimistic nature; subordinates would tell me I was very approachable, and would want a lot of attention from me, and to be my friend; and male co-workers and superiors would inappropriately approach me.) I didn't understand the distinct reactions I was getting. Then after twenty-two years of working in the corporate world, my position was eliminated due to a merger. I decided to take some time off, build some new skills, and investigate what worked and didn't work for me in my career and the careers of seventy-five other working women. This book is a result of that learning.

Forever the believer in lessons, not regrets, I traveled back in time. I reviewed each of my positions and many of my decisions and perspectives over the years. I looked for the similarities; the recurring stories in my head–an inventory of my work life.

I discovered that I was part Warrior, demonstrating

strength, courage, and confidence and part Little Girl, exhibiting humor, creativity and excitement. That was a good day. On a bad day I would exhibit righteousness, courage without focus, passion without guidance and humor without timing. I did not use the unique combination of the Warrior and the Little Girl completely to my benefit. The Warrior and Little Girl traits were wonderful and powerful in my work life, but they controlled me; I did not control them. The Little Girl would show up where she didn't serve me and the Warrior would get in the way of relationship building and satisfaction.

Over the years I would exhibit the Warrior or the Little Girl, without any consciousness of their existence. It was just my "work style," "personality," "who I was." One or the other would just show up. Sometimes it would work in my favor and sometimes not. The wrong time was always obviously wrong, things didn't work out; but why?

Co-workers would comment on my enthusiasm, my seriousness, my grace under pressure, my playfulness, my strength, my kindness; as well as my defensiveness, toughness, stubbornness, and show of emotion. I studied hard to achieve balance. Always the student, I would take workshop after workshop and read book after book to try to discover why after all these years I still didn't feel great about work.

Then came the break. I began interviewing and surveying other women about the personality characteristics that worked and didn't work for them; and I found amazing

3

similarities across the board.

Of the more than 75 women interviewed, I discovered Warriors and Little Girls everywhere in some combination; mostly used at the wrong times; almost always unconsciously. There were 100% Little Girls with no Warrior and little credibility. There were 100% Warriors with little personality and no joy. Worst of all I discovered women who had left their Little Girls behind. What was left was incomplete Warriors who lacked critical Warrior components that would make them whole, powerful and successful. In that research, five characteristics for the Warrior and five for the Little Girl emerged.

What would it look like if we were conscious of their presence and their power, cultivated them to their best expressions, and called them forth when they would be most useful? These ten traits, if developed, called upon consciously, and used for specific outcomes, could bring success **and** fulfillment.

This is a development of that possibility; the Warrior and the Little Girl. It is about discovering the values of each, and using those traits to free you from the corporate chains and games that have bound you.

It's about duality. Two equally valuable sides to your personality that can be explored, developed and capitalized on to create happiness and success at work. Hatha Yoga, a practice to strengthen the body and free the mind, represents this as sun (ha) and moon (tha). This is the masculine and feminine that combined creates a powerful balance in life.

Doc Feldshuh, my childhood doctor who is long since gone, worried 40 years ago whether his daughter could be a doctor and still retain her femininity. Could she act like a woman or did she have to act like a man in order to be accepted? Perhaps that question was necessary 40 years ago when a woman in medicine or business was a rarity, and in order to fit in, we felt we needed to act like men. Today, women are 50% of the workforce. Men are no longer the majority.

This book is for women who want to be comfortable in the workplace as women. It's for women who want to capitalize on what's instinctively there and create their most powerful and fulfilled self.

This book helps you discover who you are and who you want to be. It's about learning where your strength comes from. How you create curiosity and excitement. It is a book about balance and the scales of strength and vulnerability, knowledge and curiosity, reserve and excitement.

Remember these points as you begin the journey of discovering your Warrior and your Little Girl.

1. They are two distinct beings living in one body. They are not one personality combined. You may sometimes come from one or the other, or a combination of the two. But, they are two powerful forces, each with a unique gift for you to open as you choose.

2. They reflect your natural self: untapped ways of being that have been buried, ignored, misused or undervalued. You are not creating a different person. You will still be recognizable, only powerfully so.

3. If something you are experiencing doesn't feel right, it probably isn't. Trust your instincts. As you go through the exercises, try to distinguish the small discomfort from trying something new, from an approach that just isn't you. If it just isn't you, keep playing with the exercise until you connect with what works. It's not the destination that's not working; it's the path you are choosing.

4. While there are ten defined traits, this is a personal and unique journey. You get the most out of this if you apply it directly to who you are, and your experiences.

You can have both success and fulfillment if you cultivate your Warrior and Little Girl and use them to your benefit. It is inside of you and it's been there all this time. Don't run from the corporate environment, run to it and help change what we've helped it to become.

Chapter One

The Journey of Change

Writing this book was not an easy journey. My positive view on regrets was challenged at times as it became clear to me the many decisions and actions that were made by my over-zealous Warrior or unharnessed Little Girl. For all my Little Girl wonder, she was sometimes naive. For all her trust, she was sometimes vulnerable. For all her passion, she was sometimes defensive. For all my Warrior's courage, she was sometimes reckless. For all her integrity, she was sometimes righteous.

Here's why I have written this book. I spent 22 years in the corporate world and felt misplaced most of that time. I was successful, reaching the executive level (VP) by the time I was 35 and ultimately making a salary in the top 5% for women in the U.S. And, I was mostly unhappy.

As I moved further and further up the corporate ladder, my feelings about being there became worse and worse. I had gotten the corner office and the price was not worth it to me. I was becoming someone I didn't want to be in order to survive. My values, beliefs and rules were being violated over and over again, and I was letting it happen. What I wanted to do was find a way to thrive in the corporate world, and enjoy it at the same time. I didn't want success in the way that seemed necessary: a work life of battles, deception, long hours and lost values. The cost was too high.

I've discovered many other women who don't want success in that way either. It's no wonder women-owned businesses are growing at a rate of twice the national average, as women leave the corporate environment to find more satisfaction from their work. The sad part is they feel they must leave in order to have the experience they desire. We don't have to leave. We need to develop the best of what we are and get our success and fulfillment from the inside out.

In order to have this change, you need to change. As simple as it sounds, in order to adopt the Warrior and Little Girl, you need to clearly understand them both, and yourself. What does that mean? While you can begin to become aware of the distinction between the two, and the traits of each, you won't be able to successfully use them until you have determined how they show up for you now and how you want them to show up in the future. I recommend you read the entire book once and then go back to begin to incorporate it into your life.

And, to know yourself, you need to wake up. You need to stop going through the motions; turn off automatic pilot. Develop an honest relationship with yourself and get to know who you are today. What is that person really like? What motivates you? What doesn't work? All of these questions support you in discovering where you are right now. Knowing where you are is the only way to really know how far it is to where you want to go.

Change is scary. In fact, there is an entire, thriving industry around managing change. It can seem overwhelming and that overwhelm can keep you stuck. But it doesn't have to be that way. Take one step at a time. Change is transitional and can be done at your own pace. As you move through to the other side, it will be worth the effort. In the end, your Warrior and Little Girl will be powerful partners in your success. But you must take the first step.

THE CHANGE LADDER

On the following page is the Change Ladder. It's a pictorial of the climb you are about to begin. Its four stages are simple to explain, yet powerful to experience.

1. "You don't know what you don't know" or "unmindful with bad results" stage. This is where you are now. This means things may not feel right, but you don't know why.
2. You will soon become very aware of how much you don't know as you enter the "you know what you don't know" or "mindful with bad results" stage. This is the most difficult stage. You'll be aware of the mistakes you make and your learning will be retrospective. You will need to learn the art of compassion. Do not beat yourself up. Instead, cheer yourself on because the best is yet to come.

9

3. You will soon enter the "you know what you know" or the "mindfulness with good results" stage. This is where you are able to consciously integrate the work into your life; you'll just need to remind yourself about it.

4. Eventually you will enter the "you don't realize how much you know" or the "unmindful with good results" stage. You are unconscious with your integration. The work has just become part of who you are. You won't even need to "call" upon your Warrior or Little Girl. They will just show up, only now at the right moments. That is the power of this work.

The
Change Ladder

Unmindful with good results

Mindful with good results

Mindful with bad results

Unmindful with bad results

The secret is, you already have this ability inside of you. You will be capitalizing on your greatest potential. This is not to say it won't be uncomfortable and you won't have ups and downs. You will. It is a journey and your highs and lows will be challenging. This is normal.

The most significant aspect of this work is that you will become aware of yourself; perhaps for the first time. The discomfort will be in establishing this new relationship, getting to really know yourself, and taking charge of who you want to be in the world.

Don't put this off, but approach it at your own pace. There is no hurry. You have made the decision to discover more of who you can be and that is a fantastic first step. Don't make it a sprint. Make this a jog where you have time to take some breaths, look at what's around you, and pick the approach that's best for you. Think about more than the destination. Pay attention to the journey.

A student went to his meditation teacher and said "My meditation is horrible! I feel so distracted, or my legs ache, or I'm constantly falling asleep. It's just horrible!" "It will pass," the teacher said.

Soon after, the student came back to the teacher and said "My meditation is wonderful! I feel so aware, so peaceful, so alive!" "It will pass," the teacher said.

11

One more important thing to note is that no matter how many books you read, you will not be perfect; no one is, and no one book tells the whole story. At the end of The Warrior and the Little Girl, you will be aware and know yourself. You will see yourself for who you are, who you want to be, and where you get derailed from that goal. You will catch yourself earlier, before you get too far down the line that you can't recoup. You will discover your power and your joy. And that is the ultimate success.

You bought this book because you're looking for something. Try this on and see if it fits. An open mind leaves room for growth. You have the Warrior and Little Girl inside of you. You need only to be aware of who you are, what makes you tick, and how to use them to your best advantage. Take control and use what's best in you. Together we can change the workplace for women so that we belong based on who we are, not who we need to be to survive. We can thrive.

> *"You must be the change you want to see in the world."*
>
> *Mahatma Gandhi*
> *Indian spiritual & nationalist leader (1869 - 1948)*

Chapter Two

Get to Know the Real You

Before embarking on who you want to be, let's discover who you are today. That means deep down; not just on the surface. This is not easy. In fact, it may be a little painful. You may discover parts of yourself you don't really like. For you to grow, you need to get clear about who you are and who you are not. Clarity is a key component for growth. Clarity about where you are, about where you're going, and about the values that guide you.

We are our values, our principles and our rules. What's important to us and what we believe in guide our actions. Everything we say or do comes from these core values and these values and rules are our personal choices for how we like to live our lives. They are at our very core, conscious or not.

Many of us pretend to be something or someone we aren't in order for ourselves and others to see us the way we want to be seen; or, to merely survive a bad environment. But, no matter how much you try to fool yourself, it won't work. You can not fool your core authentic self and while the truth may not show up as awareness, it will show up somehow, usually as mistakes, bad decisions, regrets and/or unhappiness.

NANCY

Nancy, a successful, beautiful and personable woman, had many things in her life but she was not completely happy. She was living the life she thought she wanted, imagined and expected, but knew something was missing. She was overwhelmed, stressed out, unhappy, fearful and angry as we embarked on several values exercises to help her come in contact with the real Nancy.

We began our work by getting to know her. What made her happy? What did she think was the greatest accomplishment of her life? What was yet to be done? Through several exercises over several weeks, we discovered Nancy's values of feeling alive, courageous, beautiful, adventurous and free, and what each of them meant to her. We began to map how these values are played out in her life. What does she do to feel alive? What's the last courageous action she took? Where is there beauty around her? The map was small. There was not a lot of evidence of her values' presence.

She could not believe that she felt so strongly about these values yet let so many of them slip away. It was astonishing to her that she wasn't living them and that many of her decisions were counter to her values. This became the basis of our work. Anything and everything we did together was connected back to her values. If she came up with a new idea, we'd look to see if it fit in her value system. If she was having a particularly bad week, we'd look to see what values were being compromised.

Write these thoughts down.

_____

_____

_____

_____

_____

_____

Circle the words that stand out for you and write those words below.

_____   _____

_____   _____

_____   _____

_____   _____

Which two people inspire you? Why?

1.

_____

_____

_____

_____

2.

_____

_____

_____

_____

Circle the words that stand out for you and write those words below.

_____   _____

_____   _____

_____   _____

What are your favorite things to do? Why?

_____

_____

_____

_____

Circle the words that stand out for you and write those words below.

_____   _____

_____   _____

_____   _____

If you could do any job at all, what would it be? Why?

_____

_____

_____

_____

Circle the words that stand out for you and write those words below.

_____   _____

_____   _____

_____   _____

What is something that you MUST have in your life, the lack of which would make your life incomplete?

_____

_____

_____

Circle the words that stand out for you and write those words below.

_____   _____

_____   _____

19

Take a look at what you've written. What stands out?

_____

_____

_____

What words have you circled? Pick the 5 most important words that capture what is at the core of your being. Are those the words you want to use or are there better ones? Is there a better way to describe those values? *Once you decide on the words, write them down.*

_____   _____

_____   _____

_____

These are the values that are most important to you. They need to be present in your life in order for you to be fulfilled. Remember these as we move forward to your Warrior and Little Girl. Make sure you don't compromise your values. Consider those values as you navigate through the rest of the book.

Take some time to reflect on what you've just discovered. Take it in. Really accept that's who you are and what's important to you. Take time to get to know this person, if you don't already. Being this person will help bring you fulfillment.

WHAT IS YOUR WORK STYLE?

These are the questions I asked to more than 75 women who participated in the study. Think about your answers before writing them down. If you are stuck, think about a particular time when something you did worked or didn't work. What were the circumstances? What was it that affected the outcome?

What personality trait has worked well for you in your career? Why? *Write these thoughts down.*

_____

_____

_____

_____

_____

What personality trait hasn't worked so well for you? Why? *Write these thoughts down.*

_____

_____

_____

_____

_____

What childlike quality do you bring to work (if any) that has worked well for you? Why? *Write these thoughts down.*

_____

_____

_____

_____

_____

What quality do you bring to work that hasn't worked well for you? Why? *Write these thoughts down.*

_____

_____

_____

_____

_____

What trait do you wish you had that would make you more successful? *Write these thoughts down.*

_____

_____

_____

_____

Take a look at your answers. Circle the words that
stand out. What do you notice? What is occurring for you
based on your values and the personality traits you exhibit
in the office? Are there conflicts? Differences?

Write those thoughts down.

_____

_____

_____

_____

_____

_____

_____

The most powerful place for you is if your personal
and work values don't conflict. If they do, you've just discovered an important disconnect; one that affects the feeling of fulfillment in your work.

You now have a basic understanding of who you are
today and what's important to you. Keep thinking about
this as we continue. It's time to move on and create who
you want to be. A leopard may not be able to change its
spots but the beauty of being human is, we can. We can
reflect, change, and recreate.

Before embarking on identifying and enhancing your
own Warrior and your Little Girl, you must first have an

understanding and a general picture of each one. What comes to mind when you think about Warriors? Little Girls? What are the characteristics of each? You are beginning an exciting and powerful journey, full of insights and opportunities. Take a stand right now for growth. Set your intention to create what you want.

Buddha, 2500 years ago, sat under the bodhi tree and refused to move until he saw the truth. For 45 years the Buddha studied and taught his simple view of life without suffering. Your commitment will not take starvation, release of all material goods or the wearing of an orange robe. It will take the desire to look at what works and what doesn't work for you in the area of business, to authentically see your successes and places of learning, and to come face to face with who you are so you can become all you want to be.

Two monks were washing their bowls in the lake when they saw a drowning scorpion. One monk scooped it up and set it upon the bank. When he did that, he was stung. He continued washing his bowl and again the scorpion fell in. The monk saved the scorpion and was again stung.

The other monk asked him, "Why do you continue to save the scorpion when you know it's nature is to sting?"

"Because," said the monk, "to save is my nature."

Chapter Three

The ABCs of the Warrior and the Little Girl

Over 75 women took part in my survey and/or interviews. Over 1,200 years of combined experience. Almost 40% make well over $100,000 per year. Over 40% had titles of Director or above and Industries ranged from Accounting to Telecommunications. It is a well-rounded view of many levels of success, many experiences and many industries. Despite the title, industry and salary differences, the feelings and experiences were similar across the board.

They were asked what personality traits worked and didn't work for them? What childlike quality did they bring to work? What trait did they wish they had, to be more successful? The results were interesting, and not very different, regardless of their level of success.

One important thing to note is THIS IS NOT ROCKET SCIENCE. In fact, that's the beauty of it. A student once asked his teacher, "Master, what is enlightenment?" The master replied, "When hungry, eat. When tired, sleep." Instinctively, you already know more than you think you do and you already have this inside of you. You're just not in control yet. I must add, while this is not

Geri Rhoades

rocket science, it won't be easy. You will be digging deep inside yourself. Have patience and compassion and know it is all in the spirit of your future.

Below is a list of words. Check whether you think it's a Warrior trait or a Little Girl trait.

Characteristic	Warrior	Little Girl
Assertiveness		
Bravery		
Courage		
Dreamer		
Excitement		
Fun		
Grace		
Humor		
Integrity		
Joy		
Knowledge		
Love		
Magnetism		
Nerve		
Opportunity		
Possibility		
Quizzical		
Receptive		
Self-Management		
Truth		
Upright		
Vision		
Wonder		
X-chromosome		
Y-chromosome		
Zest		

Fairly easy, yes?   Again, it's not that we don't know this. It's that we don't use this. We don't make the distinction between the two and we don't call these characteristics up when they would best serve us. The power is in how they are used, how they show up, and timing. It's not that hard. Here are the answers.

Characteristic	Warrior	Little Girl
Assertiveness	X	
Bravery	X	
Courage	X	
Dreamer		X
Excitement		X
Fun		X
Grace	X	
Humor		X
Integrity	X	
Joy		X
Knowledge	X	
Love		X
Magnetism	X	
Nerve	X	
Opportunity	X	
Possibility		X
Quizzical		X
Receptive		X
Self-Management	X	
Truth	X	
Upright	X	
Vision	X	
Wonder		X
X-chromosome		X
Y-chromosome	X	
Zest		X

OPRAH

One of the most shining examples of a woman who has a beautiful Warrior and Little Girl combination is Oprah Winfrey. Oprah, born in Kosciusko, Mississippi to very humble beginnings, began life with her grandmother, moved at age six to Milwaukee with her mother and ended up in Nashville with her father. She did not fold the hand that life dealt her and had the courage to follow her dreams, the confidence to know there was more for her and the strength to stay the course. Her Warrior wouldn't have it any other way. She has ruled the airways since 1986 and is the first African-American woman to become a billionaire.

But it was her Little Girl which made us love her. After Oprah graduated from Tennessee State University she took a news anchor position in Baltimore, MD. According to Professor Deborah Tannen, author of The Argument Culture, "she lacked the detachment to be a reporter. She cried when a story was sad, laughed when she misread a word." She was offered a morning show and found her niche.

She excitedly gives away cars to her audience, has fun with her guests, cries at their pain. She travels far to help children, is curious about the world, believes in the goodness of people and knows that a smile goes a long way. Her heart is as big as her wallet; her humor as strong as her intelligence.

She is generous, kind, loving, courageous, bright, and full of integrity and honesty. She is the successful combination of the Warrior and the Little Girl. The Warrior and the Little Girl brought her success and satisfaction and a reputation many of us only dream of.

ANITA

The Body Shop founder Anita Roddick interviews a prospective franchisee with curious questions such as "What is your favorite flower?" or "How would you like to die?" This self-proclaimed rule breaker believes in possibility and she attributes that belief to the success of most entrepreneurs. "Entrepreneurs have this pathological optimism. They never see a problem," she offered at the 2004 International Coaching Federation's annual conference in Quebec.

Today with over 1,300 stores in 46 countries, Ms. Roddick is one of the five richest women in England. She has successfully combined business with heart and has capitalized on her never-ending belief in possibility.

There are others. Some whose Warriors lead the way, some whose Little Girl comes in first. That is an important call depending on who you are, your corporate culture, who your audience is and the safety of your environment. Eleanor Roosevelt had an incredibly strong external Warrior which has shaped the way we view her. According to the first lady section of whitehouse.gov, "her integrity, her graciousness, and her sincerity of purpose endeared her personally to many–from heads of state to servicemen she visited abroad during World War II." But if you read her speeches or some of her more popular quotes, you'll find a Little Girl who believes in possibility, curiosity and humor. "Life was meant to be lived, and curiosity must be kept alive. One must never, for whatever reason, turn his back on life." She also offered "the future belongs to those who believe in the beauty of their dreams."

Why have both? Can you be successful with only a strong Warrior? Perhaps. It does depend on your definition of success however. If your goal is to get ahead, and you don't care if the journey is fun and exciting filled with humor and joy, that may be the way to go. However, it's your Little Girl who brings you joy and excitement and lightness. It is the combination of the Warrior and the Little Girl, like the sun and the moon; maybe not 50/50; but a blending none-the-less that makes your work a fulfilling experience. The Warrior helps you navigate the corporate jungle. The Little Girl feeds your soul and gives you personality.

As we delve a bit deeper and discover the Warrior and the Little Girl in you, learn to value what they have to offer. If you don't, you can not expect to be able to incorporate them into your life. You too can develop both of these sides and learn when the best time is to bring them forth. The Warrior and the Little Girl, much like your values, come from your heart. Remember your values as you take this journey.

Chapter Four

The Warrior and You

The Warrior Goddess Athena sprang from the head of Zeus, in full armor, with great power. The story goes that her father, Zeus, the God of War, was warned that any children he had by Metis would eventually destroy him. Metis became pregnant, and Zeus swallowed her; resulting in a terrible headache. I would imagine that could do that to you.

Hephaestus, the God of Fire, split Zeus' skull with an ax and lo and behold, out came Athena, fully grown. Athena's mother Metis, the Greek Goddess of wisdom, bestowed upon her daughter her quality of intellect. The combination of war and wisdom, strength and knowledge, made her a formidable force and a Zeus favorite.

What was amazing about Athena was the combination of matriarchal and patriarchal elements of her being. While she was caring, insightful and reflective, she was also courageous, decisive and victorious.

According to historian Annie Ortengren, "the great goddess of wisdom, strength and reflection is a symbol of matriarchal strength. Athena represents a pyramid of stability where the base of her Warrior instincts, strategy and aggression flow into her benevolence, skills and eventually her intellect."

Not a bad description of yourself if you can get it.

Much has been written about the Warrior over the centuries. Once reserved for the man engaged in warfare, the Warrior has taken on contemporary icons such as Bruce Lee, Warrior politicians, corporate Warriors, weekend Warriors, Warrior dieters. We should collectively thank Russell Crow and Brad Pitt for giving us a beautiful vision when we think about Warriors today!

Although Athena's legend began a long time ago, the term Warrior has not traditionally been attributed to women. However, today's definition has opened the doors to a wider audience. If you look up the word Warrior in an old dictionary, you'll find "a man engaged or experienced in warfare; a champion." A more contemporary definition is a person who shows or has shown great vigor, courage, or aggressiveness. Warrior no longer needs to be a term saved for men or war.

LOZEN

Lozen, an Apache Woman born during the 1840s, fought enemies for almost forty years. Taught by her brother, she was quite clear at an early age that the traditional route of an Apache woman was not for her. Her insight, intuition, spiritual power, healing abilities and great strategic mind provided her an equal place next to the men in the war councils. For almost forty years she fought, eventually losing the battle against the U.S. Army as well as to tuberculosis, at approximately 50 years of age.

Peter Aleshire in the The Story of Lozen, Apache Warrior and Shaman offers, "The enigmatic figure of Lozen provides a link to an ancient world with surprising relevance to modern readers. For one thing, her ability to excel in a brutally male-dominated setting provides a way to examine a whole set of alternatives for women."

You don't hear much about Lozen but her story is fascinating, and can not be given justice in this short space. What is important are the Warrior qualities of courage, strength and wisdom that gave her a seat at the table, and enable us to know, that we can sit there too.

There are many very famous warrior women, or in reality, many famous women who have strong external Warriors. Senator Hillary Clinton, Eleanor Roosevelt, Susan B. Anthony, Margaret Mead, Helen Keller, Margaret Thatcher, Gloria Steinem, Condoleza Rice. Whether contemporary or historical, the list goes on. In fact, many famous and successful women are described by their Warrior traits–Eleanor Roosevelt's remarkable character, Harriet Tubman's courage, Helen Keller's strength, Madam Curie's knowledge. Your Warrior not only will give you the traits to be successful, but also give you a way in which to showcase yourself to the world.

The amazing news is that your Warrior is instinctual. You were born with the right and the power to call her forth. She has been held back by societal beliefs of the role of women and the stifling of the Warrior woman in the business world. She is powerful beyond compare and she lives inside each and every one of you.

Whether it is the inner Warrior, the inner spirit, or that guiding force that gives you strength, it's time to meet your Warrior. Connecting with this essence will bring you peace, credibility, and courage. You will find your Warrior from the top of your head to the tips of your toes, and everywhere in between.

It will be a unique connection you will have with your Warrior; a connection you'll develop over time. How you bring her forward, the role she plays in your life and the difference she'll make will be an alliance developed between the two of you. She is there to serve you and you will be grateful for her presence. Grateful for her ability to give you strength, to glow from within and shine on all you do.

There are many firsts we remember in life. The first time nature took my breath away: atop the Rocky Mountains. The first time something man-made took my breath away: walking through the Acropolis in Greece. The first time I realized unconditional love: the day my son Stephen was born.

Like the birth of a child, the birth of your Warrior can be a moving experience. When you come face to face with this powerful part of you, not only may it take your breath away, you may realize you can breathe more freely from now on.

ANNIE

My first encounter with a Warrior was my grand-mother Annie. Tall for a women of that time, Annie stood 5'8". She had violet eyes, a strong stance, a fierce resolve and determination beyond compare. No one would compromise her values or tell her something was not possible; not even her mother who told her at thirteen, when she was diagnosed with breast cancer, that she would never have a husband or dance again.

She danced in the fields before the diagnosis and danced in the fields after the successful surgery. She posed for pictures with confidence and abandon, even with only one breast. Arms spread wide, she welcomed all to see her badge of courage, an experience she wouldn't let stop her.

Not only did she have a husband but after several miscarriages, she had children; my mother and my uncle. She lived a long life and was an inspiration to many around her.

I didn't realize my grandmother had such a strong Warrior side until I got older. She simply was Nanny, who never let anyone hurt me, never let me think I wasn't the greatest and most capable, and never let me give up. She is a wonderful vision of a real-life Warrior and one I carry with me daily.

In a powerful book on the philosophies of Bruce Lee, author John Little offers this about your Warrior; "Most of us in the West have neglected our Warrior force, ignoring its presence and forgoing even the attempt to connect with it. The end result is that we end up becoming far less than we are fully capable of."

You are no longer ignoring. You are no longer neglecting. You can and will become all you are fully capable of being.

Chapter Five

The Top 5 Warrior Attributes

Warriors have many attributes and in the end, what yours will look like is yet to be seen. Through the survey and interviews, consistent Warrior traits emerged that have been particularly helpful in women's careers. With this information, combined with other Warrior research, five characteristics have been chosen that make up a powerfully-developed Warrior.

The path of the Warrior is not to be taken lightly. You will see that these attributes are not easily mastered and incorporating them into your life will take a commitment. It will require a desire to hold them dear; work to be them, and dedication to adhere to them, even in the face of non-Warriors.

Over the course of humankind, obstacles to what is good and just have been everywhere. You will need to see the value these characteristics bring to your life in order to dedicate the time and energy it will take to build them and to keep them present. If you choose to continue this path, your Warrior is already coming alive.

THE 5 WARRIOR TRAITS

COURAGE; INTEGRITY (honesty); KNOWL-EDGE; SELF-AWARENESS (self-management); STRENGTH (grace) are our Warrior attributes. Inside some of these are other characteristics we'll investigate; such as honesty as part of integrity and grace as part of strength. However, it is not choosing among them, it is a combination of the five. Having courage does not make you a Warrior if you do not have the grace that comes with strength. Being honest does not make you a Warrior, if you do not have the knowledge to support your words. Let's look at what each of them means and how some of the surveyed women experience their power.

In later chapters we delve further into each and work on building these Warrior traits. Think about your values work from Chapter 1. What values do you hold that help support your journey?

Courage
Integrity
Knowledge
Self-Awareness
Strength

At last count, Amazon.com offered 90,677 books about courage. It is the trait most often listed as necessary for leadership. It's the trait many of us think we don't have, wish we did have, and believe we can't have. It is often collapsed with our feelings of fear, as we believe if we have fear, we do not have courage.

Franklin Delano Roosevelt, a great man and president,

once said "We have nothing to fear but fear itself." He was talking about unjustified terror. The type that stops us from moving forward. This is all too common.

As courage varies between cultures as well as people, an exploration of its definition to others, as well as to ourselves, is warranted. The most powerful definition of courage is that from Mark Twain: "Courage is resistance to fear, mastery of fear - not absence of fear." Fear is part of being human and understanding this is the first step in discovering your own courage.

Leaving the corporate world and starting my own business was one of the most courageous things I've ever done. I can not even begin to tell you about the many sleepless nights, days of doubt, money fears, fears of not having anything to contribute, fears on not being able to go back if I changed my mind; and the list goes on. I was so afraid. Yet, I was very clear of my values and what I wanted. That gave me courage to keep going. And, I was willing to take the risk. I could see it was worth it.

There are stories of firemen with the courage to go into a burning building; Holocaust survivors who found extraordinary strength to survive; Christopher Reeve who had the courage to face each day with the optimism he would walk again. There are stories of alcoholics who have the courage to walk into a room of strangers and tell their stories; battered women who have the courage to leave; people who have stayed a long time at a job and find the courage to try something new. There are different levels of courage and each person and each culture knows what activities are considered courageous.

20% of the women surveyed indicated the trait they needed most was courage or confidence. Many women collapse the two. Amy says she would love to have more confidence in her negotiation for salary and benefits. Nancy would like to have more confidence in her communication in order to get what she wants. Actually, what they need is courage to face these instances in spite of their fear. Confidence will come from the actions you have the courage to take. As Aristotle once said: "Courage is the first of human qualities because it is the quality which guarantees the others."

Adherence to a code of values is how Webster's Dictionary defines integrity. This is an unwavering commitment to honesty, fairness, decision-making based on values, truth and justice. It's not so easy to say that with many companies, once being our measure for success, being sited for illegal action.

Unlike courage, where you can point to a specific act that may have been courageous, integrity becomes a core part of one's being, a way to guide your life, a reason you can be trusted.

Each person has their definition of integrity and integrity is something that is learned as we journey through life. Based on our life experiences, we all define integrity differently but the 'standard' dictionary definition is this: integrity is honesty and decent motives in all of your decisions.

I believe I have a high level of integrity, and I've done things in my life where integrity was missing. Remember, we're not perfect. I've cleaned up those mistakes where possible and I try not to do them again. My commitment is to have integrity and I am human in my execution.

HONESTY

> "Men occasionally stumble over the truth, but most of them pick themselves up and hurry off as if nothing ever happened." Sir Winston Churchill

Honesty, an important part of integrity, is a challenge in a working world that has been influenced by fear, abuse of power, limited opportunity in a challenging job market, a number of dishonest people around us, and overall lack of courage.

What's also lacking is an agreed upon code of conduct as it pertains to honesty. Does it mean brutally telling your truth? Is compassionate honesty a white lie? What exactly does it mean to be honest?

According to Merriam-Webster, honesty is "free from deception; truthful; genuine; real; creditable; marked by integrity; frank." Free from deception. Those are very powerful words. If we hold ourselves to perfection, having to always tell the truth to be considered honest, we can justify honesty as not being truly attainable (because sometimes we falter) and therefore, not possible.

In its most basic form, honesty is keeping your word, commitments and telling the truth. What does that mean? Do you have to provide information or personal data to anyone who asks? No, you get to choose who you share your truth with. Not everything is everyone's business. And, just because you are asked, doesn't mean they get to know. Honesty is the courage to let someone know you aren't comfortable providing that information.

Some women from the survey indicated that honesty was a trait that didn't work for them. Their stories indicated poor delivery and/or lack of knowledge or political sense. A Warrior is incomplete if there is honesty without knowledge. Without knowledge, honesty is just your opinion.

RESPECT

We can not leave the conversation of integrity without talking about respect. This is, by far, one of the most forgotten Warrior traits in the business world today. To treat others with respect is a must. To be treated with respect is a gift, not an entitlement. Respect is earned, given to you as you live the Warrior life and give respect to others.

Integrity, Honesty, Respect. Three very big words with very big benefits if you give them and receive them. No Warrior is complete without them.

Courage
Integrity
Knowledge
Self-Awareness
Strength

Knowledge is wisdom, judgement and what you learn from actual experience. It's learning it, remembering it and using it. The Warrior is learned. This does not mean you need a bunch of degrees that you got straight A's in. That means you are smart, and there isn't anything wrong with that. Smart gets you in the door; however, knowledge gets you across the room.

It's knowing how to do your job. It's understanding the company, the people and the politics. The Warrior knows the players, who has the power, and the unique 'rules' of the company. They know the products, the customers, and the competition. They know these things and can use this information in their daily work. They can talk to the CEO about the business environment and the receptionist about the latest corporate policy.

What knowledge is important for you and your career is based many times on your environment and your industry. In many businesses, golf is the game and business is done on the green. If you are part of one of these industries, golf would be on your knowledge list. You have to know what is required in your business.

SUE

Sue, a successful self-business owner, incorporates knowledge first and foremost into her entire life. "I like learning new things in general, but specifically at this juncture I desire to sharpen the knowledge/skills that I already have to help me become more fully, well, me! (Rather than starting something completely new.) I also like to gain more knowledge by paying even more attention to the world around me and learning from it; learning from example, both what I like and don't like. How can I become more of what I admire? And then, feedback! Gentle feedback from those I trust."

A very learned man went to a Zen master in order to learn about Zen. It was clear very quickly to the master that the professor was not as interested in learning about Zen as he was in impressing the master with his own knowledge. As the teacher explained, the man would interrupt him with anecdotes of his own experience.

Finally the Zen teacher began to serve tea. He poured the tea and filled the cup. He then kept pouring until the cup overflowed.

"Enough!" the man interrupted. "No more will go in."

"I see" answered the Zen teacher. "Like this cup, you are full of your own opinions and speculations. If you do not first empty your cup, how can you taste my cup of tea?"

Knowledge is also insight and experience and begins with discovering that there is something we don't understand. It is then getting curious enough to want to find out about it. Curiosity sparks the thirst for knowledge and knowledge is obtained by the desire for understanding. As Buddha said "Through zeal, knowledge is gotten, through lack of zeal, knowledge is lost."

In addition to zeal, an open mind is necessary to obtain knowledge. If you believe you know it all, there is no room to add anything else. Your cup is full.

Knowledge comes from many places and we'll investigate some of these later in the book. One thing is very true, knowledge is power. And, there's even a bigger payoff, knowledge and competence creates confidence.

Courage
Integrity
Knowledge
**Self-
Awareness**
Strength

It's not that we always have to think perfectly, it's that we have to act appropriately. This skill comes from knowing what it is that gets you off the Warrior path, and managing your responses accordingly. A combination of self-awareness and self-management is a critical component to your Warrior's success.

SELF-AWARENESS

By completing the getting-to-know-you section earlier, you now have an element of self-awareness you didn't have before. Your values can be your guide, as well as knowing the characteristics that work and don't work for you.

45

It's easy to get what I call 'hooked' during your work day. These are situations that happen that push your buttons, test your patience, and make you vulnerable to becoming the Warrior or the Little Girl in a place that won't serve you in the long run. You need to know what these things are, and you need to know how to manage your reactions.

The Warrior understands herself, knows her strengths and her areas needing improvement. She is clear on her motives. She does not have to share this information, she needs to use it. There is power in this level of self-awareness and having an honest relationship with yourself. This knowledge helps you self-manage.

SELF-MANAGEMENT

Self-management is the ability to control your actions. You may not be able to control how you feel, but you can control what you do with those feelings. There lies the power. The minute you do not manage your emotions, reactions or actions, you lose the game. In my case, my Little Girl sometimes makes a mess of things and I have some clean-up to do.

50% of the negative traits indicated in the survey can be alleviated with self-management. These include impatience, defensiveness, impulsiveness and more.

This Story is from the Sutra of Parables, told by the Buddha in a sermon:

Once upon a time, there was a turtle living in a pond. Because of the very dry weather, the pond was drying up and the turtle got out to ask for help. She saw two ducks passing by and shouted out, "Help! Would you please bring me to a pond full of water?"

"How can we help you out?" asked the ducks. "We are flying in the air and you are swimming in water."

"I propose that both of you carry each end of a piece of stick with you by your mouths," replied the turtle. Then I hold on to it at the middle with my mouth. You can then carry me to a pond full of water."

"That is a good idea," said the ducks. "We will help you . But you must remember not to open your mouth."

So, the ducks carried the turtle across the country-side toward the lake. As they passed over a village, a group of children looked at them and burst into laughter, "Look! What a funny sight! Two ducks carrying a stick with a turtle holding onto it with his mouth!"

The turtle was angry at the remark and replied, "you guys are stupid. What do you understand?" But, once she opened her month, she fell from the sky and crashed to her death.

Not very much self-management there. The turtle took her eye off the prize and got caught up in ancillary things. Her ego got in the way of her ultimate goal of getting to the pond. When things are at their worst, self-management is most important.

Courage
Integrity
Knowledge
Self-Awareness
Strength

Strength is so much more than muscle; it lives both inside and outside the body. Inner and outer strength complement and support each other, but they are quite different.

INNER STRENGTH

Inner strength is knowing and believing in ourselves. The more we know ourselves, the better we are at handling the situations that arise. We go through life with many internal struggles: of conviction; of path; of ego. These are struggles that we need to learn to deal with, process and move through. Do we have fortitude? A number of women in the survey indicated that perseverance was the trait that worked best for them.

This is not about inner peace. That is something wonderful in and of itself, and it is not the inner strength we're talking about here. Inner strength is where your confidence lives. It is the energy which gives you movement, clarity of mind and purpose.

Inner strength comes from your heart and the heart is a critical factor of the Warrior.   Our hearts help us know what is true. Our hearts guide our actions. Our hearts help form our beliefs. Our hearts give direction to our being, our desires and our power.

Inner strength consists of the knowledge of our personal power, what it feels like, what its potential is. That power is a force that has the possibility of pouring out in all you do.

OUTER STRENGTH

Outer strength is the showcase for your inner strength. How well you take care of the one body you are given, how you carry it, and what you choose to wear can help to communicate to the outside world your inner strength.

Grace, an aspect of outer strength, is how we carry ourselves. It's how we use our power. Are we gracious? Do we have kindness and courtesy? Are we forgiving to people who have slipped up? Grace is when you walk into the room and your being is your power, not your words. Grace is the gratitude you have and show for where you have gotten and your appreciation for others. Grace is what will set you apart from others. Grace under pressure is how Ernest Hemingway defined courage.

Inner and outer strength; it's the inside and the outside of your Warrior. Inner strength helps to clear your mind while outer strength helps to clear your way. They are partners, fragile without each other and in some cases, detrimental. You'll find out why in the "Warrior Confusion" chapter.

ADDITIONAL TRAITS

Interestingly enough, both Athena and Lozen were purported to have been celibate. Add that one to your list if you wish. I would never, in a million years, suggest it is necessary. Besides sending the message that we can not be powerful if there is a significant other in our lives, I do not think I would have many takers.

> *"True integrity is shown only when you have something to lose."*
> *Marie Curie*

Chapter Six

Accessing Your Warrior

Patty doesn't like the word Warrior; and I'm guessing some of you don't either. Let's just get past it for now. To help Patty get past the word itself I asked her to think of a woman she admires. One who carries herself with grace and courage; who knows her job, speaks honestly and who is such a captivating leader she would follow her anywhere.

Patty thought for a moment. "Someone I admire. Someone who I'd like to be like. Someone I respect. There is this women who seems so strong and confident. She knows a lot about our organization and when she walks in the room, everyone seems to notice."

"Who is that?" I asked.

"Rose" she said.

"Wonderful. Let's find your 'Rose'."

"Really?"

"Yes, really. It's not about needing to call her a Warrior; it's about personifying her so you can call her forward as a real, powerful, living, breathing part of your personality. It's who you want to be at times. For you it's 'Rose'."

"Oh" she gratefully offered. "I'll find my 'Rose'."

There may not be a Rose that's right in front of you

like she is for Patty. You may need to think about it for some time. The point is, don't get stuck on the word Warrior if you just can't get past the fighting man on a horse or the gladiator or the killing machine. That is not our Warrior and it is the antithesis of what our purpose is. That's closer to swimming with sharks, playing like a man, and the dog-eat-dog environment we don't want to play in. So, if that's where you are, leave it behind. We are looking for that part of you that gives you strength, showcases your power and allows you to walk through life with integrity and courage.

Now, let's meet your Warrior.

VISIONING

If you agree that seeing is believing, then visioning is the perfect method to meet your Warrior. It's best if you have a partner for this exercise. Someone you trust, who can slowly and clearly read the steps of the visioning exercise to you.

1) First of all, get comfortable. Find a place where you won't be disturbed and isn't noisy. You can be seated, laying down or standing if that works. Choose your position based on who you are.

2) Once you are in position, close your eyes and take some deep breaths. Slowly breathe in and

out. Concentrate on that breath. Feel the air going into your nostrils, hold it, and let it out slowly through your mouth.

With each breath, your body is relaxing. First your toes. Then your knees. Breathe. Now your thighs. Breathe. Your stomach. Your chest. Breathe. Your shoulders. Your neck. Your eyes. Breathe.

3) As you become more and more relaxed, picture yourself standing atop a mountain and you are strong and confident. You are a leader. You are courageous. You are knowledgeable. You know yourself and are comfortable with yourself. Breathe. Just be with this for a minute or two. Embody your Warrior. Feel her power.

4) Now transport that being to a more familiar place; a place where you would want to be able to be that strong and confident person. Where are you? What are the surroundings? What colors, sounds, feelings are there? What are you wearing? How are you dressed? Breathe.

Get as detailed as you can. What does your hair look like? What is your expression? How are you standing? Where are your arms? Your hands? Really take all of this in. How do you

know you're confident? What's going on inside?
If you could say something, what would it be?

If you were to give her a name, what would that
name be if it isn't your own? Perhaps
something that encompasses who she
is for you. Say that name. What happens when
you call her name? Keep breathing.

As you hold your Warrior's energy inside of
you, imagine a glow forming around her.
Wherever she goes, the glow follows. Feel the
warmth of your Warrior's glow.

5) Slowly come back to the room. Remember all
that you have seen and felt. Remember her
name. Remember what made her feel powerful,
look powerful. This is your Warrior. Embrace
her. Call her forth when you need or want her.
She is inside of you ready to come out. All you
need to do is ask. Breathe.

*When you open your eyes, write down your Warrior
experience. Some questions to answer: What does your
Warrior look like? What is her name? Does she remind
you of someone?*

_____

_____

_____

_____

_____

_____

_____

_____

_____

_____

CONSCIOUS CREATION

Some people find that visioning isn't as effective for them as they would like. If you are one of them, creating your Warrior through your past experiences can be just as powerful.

Name women (who you know, are familiar with, contemporary or historical) who you would define as Warriors.

_____

_____

_____

_____

What is it about them you find Warrior-like?

_____

_____

_____

What are some other examples of Warrior behavior that you admire?

_____

_____

_____

In what specific instance do you believe you have been a Warrior?

_____

_____

_____

What was it about that instance that made you a Warrior? What did you look like? Act like?

_____

_____

_____

Based on your answers to the previous questions, write a description of your Warrior. What does she look like? How does she stand, sit, talk? Does she have a name?

Write these thoughts down.

_____

_____

_____

_____

_____

_____

_____

Once you have created your Warrior, and have a picture of her in your mind's eye, you can envision her at any time. Remember her name so you can greet her when she arrives.

Whether through visioning or creation, this is the first stage of your Warrior. Much like a child, this being will learn and grow and evolve into who you work to make her. The journey is just beginning. You must now build your Warrior so she becomes a complete and powerful part of you.

Chapter Seven

Building your Warrior

COURAGE; INTEGRITY; KNOWLEDGE; SELF-AWARENESS; STRENGTH.

Warning: This is an important chapter filled with exercises, questions for thought and steps for building your Warrior. If you've picked this up as some light reading at night, wait until morning.

I also suggest you read a section at a time so that you don't get into overload. Each trait deserves full attention and you deserve to take it slow. Remember, this is not a sprint, it's a journey.

WHERE ARE YOU NOW?

The five Warrior attributes and their definitions are in the table on the next page. Rate yourself on a scale of one to ten (one not present; ten always present). Get five other people to rate you as well. It's helpful to see yourself through the eyes of others because we don't always see ourselves as the world sees us.

This will be a starting point. Where are your strengths? Where do you need to improve? Take your time on this. You need to be completely honest with yourself in order to fully understand your future focus.

Attribute	Definition	Self	1	2	3	4	5	Avg
Courage	Continuing in spite of fear. Courage to tell the truth.							
Integrity/ Respect/ Honesty	Having a code of morals and values that are sound and consistently adhered to. Keeping your word. Respect of others' time and opinions.							
Knowledge	Educated; knows the ropes. Listens and gives space to others' thoughts. Takes time to understand.							
Self Awareness Self Management	Having a deep understanding of your strengths, weaknesses, needs and wants. Can control your emotions outwardly and use them in positive ways. Does not act irrationally or in a knee-jerk way.							
Strength	Inner and Outer; fortitude and grace.							
	Average							

What do your numbers look like? Are there any surprises? Are there vast differences between your thoughts and what others say? Where do you want to focus your attention? What do you want your ultimate Warrior to look like? *Write down your thoughts.*

_____

_____

_____

_____

_____

WHERE ARE YOU GOING?

You continue to build your Warrior's self-awareness characteristic with every exercise. You now need to decide where you're going.

In my own evaluation I discovered my courage and integrity were solid, but I needed work in the other areas, especially self-management. My emotions were much too transparent. I also believed that with increased inner strength, self-management would be easier. I kept the eights I received in integrity and courage and the seven I received in knowledge. While all three could be better, for this time in my life it was more important to build self-management and strength. I knew that I didn't have to concentrate on all five.

I believe I am courageous and have integrity in most occasions. Although I make mistakes, these characteristics are very much a part of me and even if I spent all of my days concentrating on other things, there seemed to be little risk that I would diminish these traits. My next step was to decide where I wanted to go. I needed to set some goals.

My intentions chart looked like this:

Warrior Trait	Now	Future
Courage	8	8
Knowledge	7	7
Integrity	8	8
Self-Awareness/ Management	6	8
Strength	7	8

I could have chosen all tens, but that's a big task. I'm not sure anyone can manage to be a ten in all of these areas, all of the time. For those type-A personalities out there, begin your work in self-management and set noble, obtainable goals. It's hard, but you can do it!

You now need to set your intentions. This chart serves as a pictorial of where you are headed. As we know, real life does not go as smoothly as it does on paper so don't get discouraged. This helps focus you but again, it's a journey. It's time for you to decide where you want to go.

> "I believe the choice to be excellent begins with aligning your thoughts and words with the intention to require more from yourself."
> Oprah Winfrey

WHAT ARE YOUR INTENTIONS?

Warrior Trait	Now	Future
Courage		
Knowledge		
Integrity		
Self-Management/ Awareness		
Strength		

You now know where you are and where you are going. Let's work at each one with some helpful ways to strengthen each trait.

CULTIVATING YOUR COURAGE

Much like the cowardly lion, you too have courage inside yourself you have yet to acknowledge. One of the biggest problems with courage is how we define it. I asked many women to name something courageous. They could all come up with something. I then asked them if they would do it. Most said no.

How do we ever expect to see ourselves as courageous if we define courage beyond anything we could possibly see ourselves doing? In the past I would think that jumping out of a plane was courageous. Yet, I would never do it. And, when I thought about not doing it, I felt non-courageous. I don't define that anymore as courageous. It's simply a choice someone else might make. It's not that you don't push yourself a bit, it's that you understand yourself and the outer limits you have chosen.

How do you define courage?

Let's go back. What have you done in the past that you consider courageous?

_____

_____

_____

_____

What is something that you didn't do in the past that you would have considered courageous?

_____

_____

_____

_____

What are some things others have done that you consider courageous?

_____

_____

_____

_____

ALICE

"I've often wondered, if you go through something or do something to change your 'lot in life' and you don't know it's doing a courageous thing or being courageous, or even have a choice in the matter…is it still courageous?" offers Alice, a marketing director. "Does it still count if you went into it 'with your eyes closed'? I now say yes, and why not? The fact is, you did do it, or lived it, or survived it, and it should be recognized. I think every human being on earth, especially the underprivileged, who just get up in the morning and live their lives for another day, is courageous. I think someone who has lost a loved one and trudges through another day without them, is courageous. I think doing something you've always wanted to do and following your dreams, is courageous. I think just about anything, big or small, that is done that is not normally done because of fear for one reason or another, is courageous." Alice's generous definition of courage allows her to acknowledge many courageous moments in her own life.

GET TO KNOW YOUR RISK TOLERANCE

Courage is perhaps the most difficult attribute to build because it involves risk. Its mere definition of "doing something in spite of your fear" confirms there are obstacles right from the start.

Paula, a job placement coach, is one of the 21% of the women surveyed who wish they had more courage/confidence. For her, it's "the ability to act on one's passions, without fear. I believe if I could 'kick up' my risk-taking comfort a notch or two, then I could achieve the next step in my career." Paula understands that her fear of risk has been an obstacle for her career advancement. If she works on this, who knows where she could go next?

There is power in understanding how risk-averse you are. Take the simple quiz on the next page. What is your tolerance for risk?

Obviously, the more yes answers, the more risk-averse you are. You will need to build your courage muscle slowly and celebrate all your wins, big or small. In order to take more risks, you need to suspend your fear of what could go wrong, and focus on what could go right. The poet T.S. Eliot said it best. "Only those who will risk going too far can possibly find out how far one can go."

Geri Rhoades

THE RISK TOLERANCE QUIZ

	Yes	Sometimes	No
I need to know the outcome of events. No uncertainty for me.			
Making decisions is scary for me.			
I like to take the role of follower and let someone else lead.			
I speak up at meetings only when officially asked my opinion.			
I don't deliver anything that hasn't been asked for because it might be the wrong thing.			
Glory in the long run is not worth some short-term discomfort.			
I prefer to make decisions that cause little disruption to my work life.			
Making sure no one thinks badly of me is most important.			
I can't make any mistakes in the short-term even if I believe it will work out in the long run.			
I worry a lot about making decisions.			
Total			

66

See yourself as courageous

Courage is not always just what you do, it's also how you feel. Let's again do some imagining. Close your eyes and picture yourself as courageous. How are you different than you are now? What do you look like? How do you walk? What would you be like day-to-day, that is different than you are now?

_____

_____

_____

_____

Start small

The key to building your courage is to start small. If you consider yourself basically a non-courageous person, don't walk into your boss's office and let him know what you think of him. That would be child-like anyway; and more about that later.

Step one in building your courage is to do it reasonably. What could you do today that challenges you just a bit?

_____

_____

_____

Now, what's the one thing you can do to make the actions you wrote above easier? For instance, if what is courageous is taking a new job, you may want to talk to some experts before making any change.

_____

_____

Seek out others who exemplify courage

Nancy would have more courage if she had more mentors; more women in higher positions that she could look up to. "They are few and far between in technology companies. They don't even have to be in the same company, but banded a bit better together to share experience, strength, etc. That would give me courage."

Many women have indicated that good mentors don't exist. Perhaps that is true if you are looking for a total package. However, if you seek mentors out who have specific traits, like courage, you can find them.

Join a group

Is there a business women's group you could join where you can seek out women with courage? Write down three possible groups and contact them by tomorrow.

_____   _____   _____

5 COURAGE builders

1) Reassess your definition.
2) See yourself as courageous.
3) Take small steps.
4) Find someone to emulate.
5) Brush off your mistakes
   and celebrate your successes.

Like starting a weight lifting program with light weights, starting your courage program with something small builds confidence. From the first challenge, you will come up with another. Jump out of the plane after you've experienced hang gliding. Experience hang gliding after you've climbed to the top of a mountain. Climb that mountain after you've hiked that trail.

Eleanor Roosevelt offered this: "You gain strength, courage and confidence by every experience in which you really stop to look fear in the face. You are able to say to yourself, 'I have lived through this horror. I can take the next thing that comes along.' You must do the thing you think you cannot do."

INCREASING YOUR INTEGRITY

Integrity as you recall, is an adherence to a code of values. In discussions about the Warrior traits, I've been asked, "don't you think integrity is difficult in business today?" Difficult? Yes. Impossible? No. It is a choice. You must be willing to have integrity even though others may not; you must be prepared to be honest, although others may not; and you must learn how to identify whom you can trust. While integrity is a lifetime commitment, there are certain steps you can take right now towards increasing the presence of integrity in your life.

Conduct an integrity review of your company

To have integrity present, you must first ensure you are in the right place and doing the right job. Integrity shows up in the majority of company mission statements but many people will say it doesn't live in their environment. Sometimes there are places that just don't live up to their integrity value, or don't have it as a value at all. That is their choice. Your choice is to pick who you want to work for and with. This takes courage. You may need to move on, depending upon how important integrity is to you.

On the next page are a few questions to get you started in having the integrity conversation with yourself. Although there are only a few questions, they are not easy to answer and require some thought. Make sure you understand your own integrity rules before applying them to others.

THE INTEGRITY QUIZ

Do you believe the company you work for has integrity?	Yes	No
Is there something about your current position, the duties you perform, or the person you report to, that challenges your desire to have integrity?	Yes	No
Is there anything you need or want to do about your answers to 1 and 2?	Yes	No

Always check your own motives

This is a big challenge. It takes a combination of knowing your values and being willing to be honest. Ask yourself these questions. Why are you doing what you're doing? Is there a reason beyond the one you are telling yourself?

Keep your word.

Do what you say and say what you do. Don't just say what others want to hear if you have no intention of following those words. You may get away with that in the short-term but you will be found out in the long-term and it will affect your relationships, whether people trust you, and whether integrity is a word that describes you.

Don't promise what you can't deliver.

The best way to keep your word is to not promise what you can't or won't deliver. Keep your commitments reasonable and know that while people may be impressed with what you promise, they'll be very impressed with what you actually deliver. And, unimpressed with what you don't.

Tell the truth

Remember what we said about honesty in the previous chapter? Telling the truth does not mean spilling your guts. You need to be wise as to when and where you share your truth. Deciding what to share is your choice.

When you do choose to share, listen to your gut. You instinctively know when you are not being truthful.

This is also where rumors die. Don't start them. Don't spread them. There isn't any integrity in that and it reduces your credibility. Rumors are used many times by people who want to make others look bad for their own personal advancement.

One way you can have instant truth is in commitments. If something changes that is keeping you from delivering on a commitment you made, step up to the plate and let it be known. Make good where you can. Have the courage to tell the truth.

5 INTEGRITY builders

1) Review your company.
2) Check your motives.
3) Keep your word.
4) Don't promise what you can't deliver.
5) Tell the truth.

HONESTY

Honesty, defined as free from deception, can be challenging as white lies, secrets until the shareholders are informed, and other clichés justify the difficulty of telling the truth.

Begin with being honest with yourself

One of the safest places to begin your honesty work is with yourself. What lie have you been telling yourself that if you were honest, would make a difference? This could be big. I'll tell you one. I'm impatient because I work faster than a lot of people and I can get a lot done. LIE. My impatience is impatience and it's because I want things when I want them. It's not usually beneficial to those around me (unless things are going detrimentally slow) and it certainly isn't charming. Telling myself the truth highlights my need to work on being patient. That comes with better self-management.

Be honest with others

As said many times before, honesty is not spilling your guts. There is timing, appropriateness and motive. If honesty was easy, a large percentage of women wouldn't have indicated it was a trait that didn't work. Not everyone is interested in what you think. And what you think is not always important to the task at hand. Use a lot of self-management in the area of honesty.

Start small

If you haven't been completely honest in all of your office dealings in the past, don't start telling everything you think to everyone you know. You need to test the waters with your delivery and content to make sure what you're saying is well thought out, with purpose, and clearly understood.

Check your motives

Some people have to tell the truth so they feel better, not because it will actually help the situation. Check your motives and make sure what you're 'sharing' is actually helpful. Is it for the betterment of the team, the company or you? It's not that it can't be for you. It's that you need to know that ahead of time so you don't fool yourself into believing it's best for someone else.

Plan what you're going to say

Honesty doesn't mean spontaneous. You have a responsibility to share your truth clearly. Think it through. What is the outcome you are looking for?

Be aware of how it is being received

This means being aware of the reactions of the other person. If you are watching and listening to how someone is responding to what you're saying, it's very obvious when honesty is going down the wrong road.

Check in that it is understood

Communication is not what is being said, it's what's being heard. Stop and ask if they understand or if they have any questions. Recap what you're saying from time to time. Check in before you finish so you can ensure you haven't made a mess you need to clean up.

Is there a place when honesty is not the best policy?

13% of the women indicated that honesty was the trait that didn't serve them well. Most indicated it was a matter of timing and style. In addition to this, too much honesty without knowledge will get you into trouble every time.

MYRA

Myra, a director in financial services, has managed the timing and delivery issue after some hard lessons. "It took me awhile to understand that while I can simply call things as I see them and not assign blame to anyone, most other people assume that even constructive criticism is just a way at taking a shot at someone." She has found that the right time, place and delivery helps combat how honesty is received.

DEBRA

"Many organizations don't always want to know the truth from people. They want things to just go smoothly, which often means smoothing over or ignoring things that might invite complexity, conflict, or uncertainty," offers Debra, an international executive coach. In these instances, choosing the right words, phrases, timing and location will be a great help.

Scott Peck, the author of the very popular The Road Less Traveled, describes the journey of honesty as "a continuous and never-ending process of self-monitoring to assure that our communications—not only the words that we say but also the way we say them—invariably reflect as accurately as humanly possible the truth or reality as we know it."

KICKING KNOWLEDGE UP A NOTCH

Many years ago I had a professor who was very bright. I told him I wanted to be bright too. What did he suggest? He told me to read everything; books, articles, cereal boxes, anything I could get my hands on. I took that advice and while I don't think I'd be described as book smart, I certainly feel well versed in a number of areas and can carry on conversations on various subjects. This is not to say that I spend time talking simply to talk; that isn't so bright. As Plato once said, "Wise men talk because they have something to say; fools, because they have to say something."

As we said earlier, knowledge is not measured in the number of degrees you have, but in knowing what you need to know and applying it successfully. With so much information in the world at our fingertips, we can get over-whelmed with the possibilities.

LET'S DO A KNOWLEDGE CHECK

What type of knowledge do you use on a day to day basis?

_____

_____

_____

_____

How has this information helped you?

_____

_____

What do co-workers you admire seem to know?

_____

_____

How can you get that information?

_____

_____

If you knew what they knew, how would that help build your knowledge base?

_____

_____

WAYS TO BUILD KNOWLEDGE

1) Make a list of your gaps of knowledge for your current position and environment. Then take a course or enroll in some further education to close those gaps.

2) Read the paper every day, including the sports section. After all, you are in the room with many men and it's good to know what's going on with the home team.

3) Get a hold of the annual report as well as any marketing materials you can find from your company. Regardless of your position, you should know what makes the company successful. In addition, subscribe to, and read business journals, trade journals, etc. There are more out there than can be counted so choose wisely. See what others around you are reading.

4) Ask lots of questions. Get curious. Curiosity builds knowledge.

5) Learn to listen. There is a lot of information going on around you that can be very helpful. Spend more time listening than talking and see how much further you get.

A BIT ABOUT LISTENING

There are three levels of listening. Level one is hearing the words but thinking about what you are going to say or do next. I call that *"Hollywood Style."* That is not listening and there is very little, if anything, to gain when you are in that mode.

Level two, *"I'm all ears"* is listening to what is being said. You are present to the words and are taking in information. This is a good start and will provide you with additional knowledge. However, you are not fully present.

Level three, "*I'm all ears, eyes and heart*" is the most powerful level. At this level, you are listening to what is being said as well as what is not being said. That is being in tune with how it is being said, what's under the words, what more is there that isn't being said. This is where you get the most information.

It is very difficult to go through the entire day at level three. Not only will you experience information overload, but you will be completely exhausted. Use level three at the best times, where you need to gain the most knowledge.

There are a couple of ways to boost your listening skills.

1) When someone is communicating, repeat back to them what you think you are hearing.
2) At the end, clarify what you think you've heard.

Paula, a corporate lawyer for a large telecommunications firm finds that listening is her greatest skill. "It gives me the information I need to make powerful decisions."

DONNA

Donna finds that knowledge helps to build her confidence. When she has something she needs to do, she makes sure she prepares and knows as much as she can. Since her outward being is quiet and reflective, she's not intimidating and finds that people share information with her. She's also a very good listener, which is a great trait for building your knowledge.

---

5 KNOWLEDGE builders

1) Know your gaps.
2) Read.
3) Learn about the company.
4) Get curious.
5) Listen better.

YOUR SUBSTANTIAL SELF

There are few things more powerful than already knowing your strengths and weaknesses when others point them out. Knowing your strengths when receiving compliments adds to your confidence as you are getting confirmation for what is already believed. Knowing your weaknesses when receiving constructive feedback or even being attacked, helps diffuse the tendency to get defensive. There is nothing more powerful than being able to reply with "I know, I'm working on it" to someone who has just accused you of being stubborn.

Let's see what you know about yourself now. Below is a chart for you to list your strengths and areas needing improvement.

Strengths	Improvement Opportunities

Self awareness is not just knowing yourself, it's knowing how you occur to others. I participated in a wonderful 360° exercise where I sent an automated questionnaire to about 25 people who I had worked with, clients, friends and family. What I got back was eye opening and a bit humbling. There was a question that asked what my greatest weakness was. Nothing that came back surprised me. I can be defensive, impatient and sometimes abrupt. What did surprise me was, although I knew these things, I didn't think others did. Wake up call. People see you for how you are most of the time. You're not hiding. They know it. Even better that you know it too.

Mary, a family life educator finds that her most important personality trait has been her self-awareness. "My self-awareness shows up by having a sense of how I am behaving in relation to others; my own process; my reactions and how I process; my boundaries as compared to others; what role I plan in an interaction."

Beth, a senior executive making a six-figure salary, finds that self-awareness is also her strongest trait. "Possessing an acute sense of myself lends itself to understanding others. And understanding others, in turn, has increased my ability to read people and situations and anticipate moves. This has allowed me to stay a few steps ahead in my organization." Really understanding herself has also helped Beth not take herself too seriously. Self awareness combined with humor is exceptionally powerful.

BUILDING SELF-AWARENESS

Choose to tell yourself the truth

Easier said than done. It's painful to look at our weaknesses, places we've made poor choices, what does and doesn't work, and take responsibility; taking away the blame from others. This is a safe place. You are the only one who you are sharing this information with and so it remains private.

Check in with other people

You need to experience yourself through the eyes of others. We are often blinded by how we've seen ourselves over the years. We've changed and we aren't always aware of how those changes look from the outside. Word of caution: not every one has clean motives. To protect yourself, ask feedback from those you trust. Make sure they have your best interests at heart.

Learn to ask yourself tough questions

What are my motives? What do I hope to gain? Am I really being honest with myself?

Process events

What went right? What went wrong? What could I have done differently?

Accept responsibility

It's not that it's always your 'fault.' It's that accepting responsibility gives you the most power to change things. You can not change the behavior of others but you can change your behavior.

It may be beneficial for you to participate in assessment tools that help you understand yourself, your strengths and your areas for improvement. Do a few of these to get different perspectives. Most are available on line for a small fee. If there is something specific you are interested in, such as you as a collaborator, or you as a leader, search the web for that criteria.

5 SELF-AWARENESS builders

1) Motivational Appraisal of Personal Potential (MAPP)
2) Myers-Briggs Type Indicator
3) Emotional IQ test
4) Reflected Best Self (RBS)
5) 360 Reach

(Go to any search engine and put in these names. You will have a number of organizations to choose from.)

SELF-MANAGEMENT

Perhaps one of the biggest gifts you can give yourself for self-management is to know that everything you think and feel doesn't need (or want) to be shared. And, not everything you want to share needs to be shared at that moment. You can take time to think.

Self-management shows up in a number of ways and is a gradual process. My work took me from showing my emotion, to being able to not react so outwardly by breathing and taking some time or organize my thoughts. It really depends on the situation. Once you become aware of the concept of self-management, it's amazing how quickly you discover how little there is of it, even in the most important situations. 50% of the negative traits mentioned in the survey could be reduced with self-management.

One of my clients asked me to participate in an interview with her for a prospective new hire. She thought this woman was a great match and wanted to see if she was missing anything. She was also concerned that this person might get bored with the responsibilities.

I quickly uncovered new information. The woman has been in a new position for the past three months that she was looking to leave because she wanted more decision making responsibility.

Since this was a deal breaker for her at her current employment, I was interested in what decision making meant to her. I asked her to explain the types of decisions she had made in her previous positions. When she gave her response I asked her to describe this concept further.

She replied, rather sharply, "I already did and I would expect that someone of your level would understand decision making. But since you don't, I'll try again." Well, had this been my interview for someone to work with me, I would have let her finish her response, asked her if she had any questions, and then thanked her for coming. Instead, I remained there, smiled, and thanked her for her second explanation.

This interviewee is a great example of a wayward Warrior. She had courage (although blinded), knowledge in the way of skills and some external strength but was missing the critical attributes of respect and self-management. Anyone who has been in an interview knows that being at your best is critical and if you get thrown off easily, you must call upon your self-management in a big way.

A half-baked warrior tastes as bad as half-baked soufflé where the eggs are still raw and runny. Not fit for many palettes.

5 SELF-MANAGEMENT builders

1) Learn to breathe and take a pause. Don't respond quickly, pout, or give up your power.
2) From your self-awareness work, discover your trigger points and begin to deal with them in a more productive way.
3) Use the mantra, "I don't have to respond now." Be careful not to use this as a substitute for having the courage to communicate your position.
4) Learn to smile. What we do on the outside sends positive messages to our brain.
5) Get curious about the conversation, asking questions to understand further.

A word of caution. Some women self-manage by becoming inauthentic and manipulative. This is not about avoiding conflict, sacrificing your integrity, or giving up power. It is about regaining control of yourself so you can be the best you can be.

SOLIDIFYING YOUR STRENGTH

Strength is a combination of what you feel inside with what you show outside. This is a partnership. You need your inner strength to help create your outer strength and you need your outer strength to help showcase your inner strength.

WORKING YOUR INNER STRENGTH

Inner strength is where you get your fortitude or perseverance. 8% of the women surveyed mentioned perseverance as the trait that makes them successful. It is their ability to keep going in spite of the obstacles thrown in their paths.

In order to discover and cultivate your inner strength, you need to look inside. There are several methods of doing this including the self-awareness exercises mentioned previously. In addition, spending quiet time with yourself and investigating where your strength comes from is also helpful. Meditation is used by a number of people and may help you. Go to www.meditationcenter.com to learn more. According to them, meditation is defined as "consciously directing your attention to alter your state of consciousness." When in a quiet state, ask yourself, "Where do I feel my strength in my body? Where does it come from? Where does it travel?"

WORKING YOUR OUTER STRENGTH

Outer strength is what you show the world. It is the presence and grace with which you move through life. Grace is such a wonderful word and never referred to in a negative way. There are so many ways to ensure your new-found inner strength has a worthy vehicle in which to live. Here are just a few.

1) Practice in the mirror. What does your Warrior look like? What are your Warrior's expressions? What clothing encourages your Warrior to be present?
2) Videotape yourself during a presentation or a meeting to see how your power shows up externally.
3) Work on your handshake. Make it firm but not too overbearing.
4) Look people in the eyes when you're listening or speaking.
5) Learn to smile. A smile does not indicate weakness. It indicates confidence and comfort with yourself, as long as it's authentic.

PRACTICE OWNING THE ROOM

My mother used to tell me that when I walked into a room, I should 'own it'. That means that you walk in as if you are the reason everyone is there. Although this may sound egotistical, it's not. Your self awareness tells you it's not the real reason they're there. But, if you don't pretend that it is, you continue to walk in as a grateful visitor and your power and grace never show. Here's how you own the room:

1) Bring your Warrior into the room with you. Always own the room with your Warrior.
2) Walk in and look around the room at each person. Greet them personally. Make sure you look them in the eyes and smile as if to say "thank you for coming to my meeting."
3) Be prepared. Know what you're there for and what your role is. Do some homework.
4) Ask questions and offer comments when appropriate. You don't have to say a lot. Your outer strength is speaking for you.
5) If you have to leave early, mention that before and don't apologize while you're leaving. Simply acknowledge the meeting leader with a nod, and walk out with your Warrior.

COURAGE; INTEGRITY; KNOWLEDGE; SELF-AWARENESS; STRENGTH

What does it look like for your Warrior to be in full force; all of the pieces working together toward a common goal? This is your ultimate objective and your greatest challenge. Each Warrior trait is special and challenging on its own. Working to attain a measure of all five is a commitment. Remember, all five Warrior traits need to work together as a part of the greater whole. Again, without knowledge, honesty is just an opinion. Without integrity, courage is just bravado.

What would it look like if you were applying all five traits to a given situation? What power does the integration provide where the whole is far greater than the sum of the parts?

CAROL

Carol came to me because she was having difficulty moving on from a decision she had made regarding her next career move. It was her fault. It was her mother's fault. It was her father's fault. Although two years had passed, she still couldn't understand why she had not accepted the offered position and she certainly couldn't forgive herself. Because of her obsession with this decision, she had been unable to make another career move-due to her fear of making the wrong one. She wanted to revive her career but this 'mistake' kept haunting her.

We began working not on what her next move would be, but why she continued to hold onto "the one that got away." She made lists and lists; the 20 reasons she can't let go; what the cost is to her of holding on; the other possible perspectives on the decision (it wasn't a mistake, it was the right choice at that time). Nothing helped her change her thinking or unparalyze her from moving forward. It was time to call up her Warrior.

Carol's Warrior was buried deep inside, rarely if ever seeing the light of day. What kept that Warrior hidden was Carol's lack of courage and her tendency to blame those around her for decisions she had made. Carol needed to have the integrity to own her own decision; the grace to accept it; the wisdom it brought her; practice self-management to control her thinking and the courage to move on. A Warrior in full force. This isn't easy but it's all there. She eventually did take this approach and recently accepted a new position. She and her Warrior have moved on, together.

Think of a recent career event that didn't go the way you planned (i.e. a meeting that went poorly; a conversation that didn't result in your desired outcome; a decision you made that you regretted). Now that you know the Warrior traits, how would you handle it differently?

_____

_____

_____

_____

_____

_____

_____

_____

PRACTICE

The Greek philosopher Aristotle said "We are what we repeatedly do. Excellence, then, is not an act, but a habit." That means, practice, makes perfect. You do not have to be born a fully-functioning Warrior, you can enhance your Warrior by concentrating on the areas that need improvement. Most of our behavior is based on habits, and research shows that you can create a new habit in 21 days of practice. Think of it: 21 days from now, your Warrior might be in full force.

Where are you now?
You may be at mindful with good results in some areas but not in others.

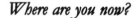

Unmindful with good results

Mindful with good results

Mindful with bad results

Unmindful with bad results

Chapter Eight

Calling up Your Warrior

Until your Warrior becomes a natural integration into your life, it's important to develop a way that you can call her forth. There are a number of ways you can invite her in.

SOMETHING TO SEE

Sometimes it helps to actually carry or post a picture of your Warrior. Whether it's a picture of you that reminds you of your Warrior self, a picture of someone you admire, or an object you can get to quickly, something visual can be a helpful reminder. Think for a moment what object you can identify that reminds you of your Warrior. If it's a real person, carry that picture around. If it's you as your Warrior, draw it or have someone take a picture of you when you are your greatest Warrior self. Or, sometimes your Warrior is so strong, you can call her up in your mind's eye.

In addition, you can post the Warrior traits in a place that you will see on a daily basis. This serves as a reminder of all the tools available to you.

SOMETHING TO DO

Some people find it helpful to 'do' something, rather than look at something, to get into their Warrior self. My Warrior is most present for me when I do my yoga practice. One of the most beautiful and strong yoga poses is that of the Warrior. The Warrior pose, named after the courageous hero Virabhadra, represents strength from the rooting of the feet to the reach of the arms. Simply by getting into this position with intention and concentration, I can begin to feel the Warrior stirring within. In this pose I become my Warrior.

This may be helpful for you as well. Stand with your feet about three feet apart. Weight is evenly distributed. Feel your feet firmly on the ground, as if roots were coming from them. Feel the roots pulling your feet into the ground.

Now, turn your right foot to a 45 degree angle and bend your right knee. This is the position of your legs. Once you feel you are grounded, that you have your balance and you are firmly cemented to the ground, lift both your arms, out to the side, to shoulder height.
The role of the arms is intention. Lift them as if you mean business. Keep your fingers straight and point them in either direction, with purpose; as if you are trying to touch each of the walls they are pointing to. What is your intention?

Turn your head to the right and look beyond your right hand, beyond yourself, to what's outside. Where are you going? Once you are grounded in where you are, you can go anywhere.

While this pose is very powerful for me in calling up my Warrior, I haven't found it useful in the middle of a meeting. People wonder what I'm doing. If I'm going to use this pose, I do it before hand. For the times you are with others and don't want to get into your Warrior pose, other tools may be helpful.

BREATHE YOUR WARRIOR IN

In yoga, the body, the mind and the breath are all connected and dependent upon each other. There is no movement without breath and the movement always follows the breath. It is interesting that something we need to do to survive, is something not many of us do well. And even if we're fairly good breathers, rarely do we use this powerful tool.

Done correctly, a breath gives you energy. A breath gives you pause. A breath gives you time to regroup, respond and rejoice.

Breath can be separated into four steps. Inhale through the nose, hold the inhale, exhale through the nose, and hold the exhale. Holding the inhale energizes the body. Holding the exhale, cleanses the body. Hold in the good, eliminate the bad. It is important to breathe slowly, deeply, and be aware of the breath. Connecting to your breathing is a key element to using it effectively. Breathing is most powerful when visualization is part of the process. As you take a breath, picture energy, power and control entering your body, filling it up. As you exhale, picture negative feelings, thoughts, emotions fleeing your body as fast as they can. Practice your breathing and you can use it to call forth your Warrior. You will feel more in control, full of power, and ready to respond to anything.

STANDING REFLECTION

There is a simple, yet powerful pose in yoga called Tadasanna, or Mountain Pose. Stand with your feet hip-width apart, toes facing forward. Your weight should be balanced, equal on both feet and equal between the toes, balls of the feet and heels. Your spine is straight, your knees are straight but not locked and your arms are at your sides. Your eyes should look forward as the top of your head reaches to the sky.

As you are in this pose, consider what it means to you. What does it take for you to stand tall? Stand firm? Stand still? Can you learn to do it with silence or do you always need to use words? Where can your body help you in this quest?

The key to this posture is to feel the rooting of your feet as you stand up tall, signifying strength and stability. At any time during the day you can get into Tadasanna and no one will know. You will simply look like you are standing tall. They will however feel the power coming from your Warrior.

WALKING REFLECTION

Walking as a form of powerful communication has been around for a very long time. The Aboriginals of Australia have a ritual they call a 'walkabout'. During this 'walkabout' a young man goes on a long journey in order to learn more about himself.

Take a Warrior walk. As you are slowly walking, picture your Warrior walking with you. How does she look differently than how you look? What is her posture? Gait? With each step you take, picture energy from the ground shooting up through your feet, into the rest of your body. Picture the Warrior by your side. Invite her in. You are becoming your Warrior. What does it feel like now?

As you walk from meeting to meeting, do so consciously and with intention. Bring your Warrior with you and walk into the room in full force.

Your Warrior will be a ray of light inside your being. While at first it may feel like a role you are playing, in time it will become an integral part of who you are. The more you incorporate her into your total being, the more naturally and easily you will be able to call her to the surface.

Chapter Nine

Warrior Confusion

THE WARRIOR AND THE BITCH

In the movie *Dolores Claiborne*, Kathy Bates as the title character says "Sometimes being a bitch is all a woman has to hold on to." While I disagree with Dolores, there are many women who don't.

In the 22 years I was in the corporate world, no one ever called me a bitch. Now that I've said that in writing, someone will come forward who thought I WAS a bitch. I get that. Situational bitchiness. We don't always do or say the right thing, especially if we need some self-management work. But these situations are very different than nasty behavior as part of your total being. So many women confuse their consistent inappropriate behavior with being a Warrior or a strong woman. Anyone you know?

Karen believes she is a Warrior. Her take no prisoners attitude, lack of integrity, disrespectful manner, use of power to forward her own agenda and gossipy nature are very far from who a true Warrior is.

Many of you have stories like this as well. Why do some women resort to this behavior instead of bringing up their Warrior? It protects them and it's easier. Cultivating or calling forth our Warriors is much more difficult and, in order to be able to be your Warrior, you have to value her. And, you have to see the distinction between the bitch and the Warrior.

The biggest distinctions are in motive and delivery. A bitch is motive without integrity and delivery without respect. That means the reason you are saying what you're saying is for your own self-interest and the way you are saying it is without kindness and respect. Are you manipulative, insulting, rude and insensitive? Are you a bully?

Julie knows that some people consider her nasty. Part of this she attributes to the requirements of her job which include putting people on performance plans, holding them to task and even letting people go. That being said, she does know that her communication style doesn't help matters. "I tend to use negative language like don't, can't, isn't. I find if I concentrate on more positive words, people respond to me better."

I have come across women who have tried to cosmetically cover up this very nasty way of being. One of the best examples is Lori. Lori knows that many people consider her a bitch. She also doesn't want to do much about it. So, instead of changing her behavior, she lets her hair grow. "It's better to be a bitch with long hair than a bitch with short hair," she said. "People respond to you better." In the end she is still considered in the same vein, but it takes her longer to do her hair in the morning. You really can't cover it up.

For the first year of writing this book, a famous

female musician was in the Warrior/Little Girl combination section. Every time I reviewed that section, I felt torn about whether to keep her there. While no doubt she has attributes of both, there is something very edgy and disrespectful about her. Her talent and perseverance has brought her millions of fans and lots of money, but I wonder if she traded some respect for her success.

Below are some characteristics of nasty behavior and the Warrior traits that could help counteract them.

Non-Warrior	Warrior
Manipulative	Honest
Mean spirited	Integrity
Short tempered	Self-Managed
Selfish	Self-Aware
Disrespectful	Respectful
Untrustworthy	Honest
Intimidating	Courageous

While there is some truth to strong women being labeled a bitch unjustifiably, it is not the only answer. If you are a woman who has been called a bitch, or your self awareness is telling you it is a qualifier you deserve, take some time to review your behavior. Are there other ways you could communicate? Are you taking the easy way out? Are your motives clean? Where can the Warrior serve you here and make a difference in the encounters you have and the relationships you seek to build?

_____

_____

_____

_____

DOES THE WARRIOR HAVE COLOR?

This book is for women, red, yellow, green, black, white, blue. Your Warrior is your Warrior. In my consulting business I came across a powerful African American woman who had some thoughts about the difference between how strong white women and strong black women are received. Up until this meeting, I hadn't thought about race. She asked me if the book was going to deal with that.

My first reaction was fear. I, by no means, am an expert on race. The Warrior is my thing. I told her that I didn't in any way want to presume to understand the race issue. I offer the Warrior to all, regardless of race. You need to try it on and see if it fits.

She gave me some good advice. "Don't presume to know us, just don't forget us." That was important. Through this meeting I had the opportunity to work with her organization, which was heavily represented by African-American women. I decided to at least pose the question to other women of color.

Wendy believes that women of color are feared more as their Warriors and sometimes that's deserved. "We come across harder, tougher, and that's hard to take." She believes this is due, in part, to having to try harder and they haven't yet found a successful balance.

"I know I walk in with a chip on my shoulder just waiting for someone to say something" offers Carole, a real estate executive. "And when they do, and I respond, they think I'm a bitch." I asked her if she was. "Yes, sometimes I am."

"The Warrior presents no more of a challenge to a black woman than she already has" offers Sara. "I have to do more than average based on being a black woman anyway, Warrior or not." So, for Sara it's more about being black than being a Warrior.

Anita agrees. "It's tough no matter. It's just another obstacle." However, she loves the word Warrior as it reminds her of the stories she's heard about her ancestors in Nigeria. She thinks there is more danger for women of color in not managing their Little Girl. "Too much Little Girl will hurt their credibility. Being black, there is an enhanced need for credibility."

According to Marlene Fine, a Simmons College professor specializing in diversity issues, "Gender is socially and culturally constructed. African American women learn to perform it in a way that is much more powerful than the way that white women do. They speak directly and are unafraid of conflict and confrontation. They face problems in the workplace because they present as Warriors--white men (and women) are often afraid of their power."

What does this tell me? Does the Warrior have color? Perhaps. The diversity issue is much more complicated than simply posing this question to a few women of color. However, the Warrior traits stand strong regardless. If color seems to be an issue for you, make sure your self-awareness is strong and you understand what gets in the way. How you deliver your Warrior needs to be based on your style, your environment and your goals. You need to determine how she needs to be adjusted, if at all. If one or more of the traits aren't working for you, modify how you show them in the world. Any organization can reject a Warrior, no matter what color, who is more like a bulldoz-er. Concentrate on understanding your organization and increasing your self-management.

ARE YOUR INNER AND OUTER STRENGTHS IN CONCERT?

If your inner and outer strengths are not in concert, you could run into trouble. Lynne's external Warrior is well developed. She walks in as if she owns the room and speaks with confidence. Therefore, she is met with equally confident people who tell her like it is, challenge her opin-ions, and fight her for a part of the room.

Unfortunately, Lynne's internal Warrior is unrecogniz-able and underdeveloped. She has mistaken her ability to walk the walk with her ability to walk the talk. Her talk, her internal talk, gives her away every time and suddenly, out comes the child to protect her. This is going to speak to many of you who have spent years developing the abili-ty to sound and look confident, yet inside you're as fragile as butter in the sun.

Masking your insecurities with an overly strong Warrior facade will result in defensiveness, argumentativeness, and frustration. This does not mean you walk around showing all of your insecurities. It means you need to temper your outer Warrior as you work on your inner Warrior. They need to complement each other to realize their full potential.

When I first met Kathy I thought she was 100% Warrior. I would observe her at meetings and she would speak with confidence and grace. She knew her facts and was skilled at communication. Externally she seemed all Warrior and therefore, was treated with equal force. As time went on I observed, sometimes first hand, her complete disrespect for those around her. When challenged or frustrated, she communicated condescendingly, reactionary and without care for others; a reaction due to under-developed inner strength. This caused her to underutilize the respectful aspect of integrity and the characteristic of self-management. These were dangerous omissions and it was reflected in the fact she had few alliances.

You can not pick and choose the Warrior characteristics you wish to have. You need all five in order to complete your Warrior self. They all don't need to be equal, but they all need to be present and available to you.

COURAGE; INTEGRITY; KNOWLEDGE; SELF-AWARENESS; STRENGTH

Chapter Ten

The Little Girl and You

When I was a little girl, I believed that if everyone just showed more love towards everyone else we would have less hunger, no wars, and the world would be a much better place. As time went on, I never stopped believing this. And, to this day, I believe it's true.

There is a Little Girl living in all of us who wants to believe that optimism and possibility will be rewarded with success; that there is a time to laugh and play and those traits will enhance, not hinder, our careers; that asking questions shows initiative, not ignorance. This is not about being the stereotypical "good girl", "nurturing girl", "nice girl". There are many strong and capable women we can point to that have retained a wonderful Little Girl as a noticeable part of their personality.

Remember my grandmother Annie, the Warrior? I have never heard a laugh like hers. Deep and infectious, she would offer it with no apologies and no turning back. Her violet eyes would sparkle when she was excited about something and her spirit would glow as warmth radiated around her. This was a woman who had withstood many tragedies yet always lived in possibility for the future. She had the most wonderful Little Girl ingrained within herself.

ELLEN

Ellen Degeneres has a magnificent external Little Girl. She dances around the stage, makes fun of herself and her guests, laughs with them, cries with them, all in a pair of perfectly clean sneakers!

She shares her Little Girl with all of us as she trusts us to be kind to her. If she didn't have that trust, she could not so freely open up. As a result, we laugh and cry with her, and we're willing to be silly with her. Each time I turn the TV on to spend an hour with Ellen, my life is uplifted. This is the power your Little Girl can have in the world.

She has a great Warrior too. Very much a public figure, she endured a very public coming out, a public breakup and an initial shunning from Hollywood. She stood tall, apologized to no one and stayed the course. This courage and integrity paid off for her and she found a home on daytime TV. Winning an Emmy for best new talk show her first year, she has reclaimed her position at the top. Her Warrior is her own and her Little Girl is for all.

Sometimes your Little Girl outwardly serves the world, like in the case of Ellen, and sometimes your Little Girl is quieter and fuels your Warrior work. Marie Curie, the only woman to win two Nobel Prizes–in physics and in chemistry–had an insatiable curiosity. She described herself as "among those who think that science has great beauty. A scientist in his laboratory is not only a technician: he is also a child placed before natural phenomena which impress him like a fairy tale."

Her dedication to her education and the pursuit of knowledge resulted in obtaining a master's degree in both physics and mathematics in only three years. Through her research she discovered Radium, said to have been the most important element discovered since oxygen. In 1903 she received, along with her husband Pierre, the Nobel Prize for physics. "All that I saw and learned that was new delighted me. It was like a new world opened to me, the world of science, which I was at last permitted to know in all liberty." Look at the words she used. Beauty, delight, a child, impressed like a fairy tale. Her words, her feelings. Her Little Girl.

It is more difficult to name famous women who have a strong, external Little Girl than it is to name women that have a strong, external Warrior. It is not that many successful women don't have Little Girl qualities, it's that they keep them safe and share them only when they feel confident it's the right environment. You need to be fully aware of your environment, the circumstances and what is acceptable. Childlike traits can be misplaced and misinterpreted such as excitement that is over the top, possibility that is blinded, play that looks careless, curiosity that looks uninformed. You need to choose when, where, and how to show your Little Girl.

The beauty of being a Little Girl as an adult is that you get to keep all that knowledge you've gained over the years. That means that you are a smarter Little Girl, a less naive Little Girl, less trusting when appropriate and necessary and all around in greater control.

This requires awareness. Believe me, any trouble I've gotten into has been from my unharnessed Little Girl. She can be defensive, pouty, needy and frustrated at times. But, I would rather manage her than give her up. My greatest joys come from what she brings me—creativity, laughter, inspiration and more. There is no joy without her and I want her in my work life. She just needs to be handled a bit differently sometimes.

In a 2002 St. Petersburg Times article, Nunzio Quacqarelli, editor of the MBA Career Guide, reported on Roselly Ramseyer-Torres, global head of equity products at Dresdner Kleinwort Wasserstein (DKW). A graduate of Harvard Business School, she is "one of the most senior female investment bankers in the world. When you meet her, she is vivacious, funny and thoroughly enjoying life. She is one of a growing breed of management-educated women working as executives, who don't just reach the top, but actually thrive and bring a new perspective to their companies."

The minute you stop believing that your job can be exciting and fulfilling, you might as well pack up and go home. For no doubt, on your deathbed, you will have many regrets. That excitement and joy, belief in the impossible, taking the time to laugh and play, that is your Little Girl. Invite her back. She will add joy and fulfillment to your work life that you thought might have been gone forever.

Chapter Eleven

The Top 5
Little Girl Attributes

For many years we have been getting advice on how to be more like a man. The promise has been that if we become manlier, we will reap the benefits of advancement, increased pay and success. Unfortunately, in many industries, these benefits have been slow in coming as women are still paid less on the dollar, have attained fewer upper management positions, and are noticeably scarce in the boardroom.

Consequently, more and more women are leaving the corporate world for something new. In studies by Catalyst (1998) and Moore and Buttner (1997), women indicated the glass ceiling, needing a work environment in line with values, lack of flexibility and feeling unchallenged at work as the key reasons for their departures. While the glass ceiling is a real and frustrating obstacle for many women, and one that can't immediately be changed, other methods of obtaining fulfillment are certainly in our immediate control.

The values work in the Get to Know the Real You chapter gave you some insight into which values you need to be present in order for your work life to be fulfilling. Which of these Little Girl traits fit those values?

THE 5 LITTLE GIRL TRAITS

CURIOSITY; HUMOR; EXCITEMENT; PLAY AND POSSIBILITY were the most noted Little Girl traits that brought fulfillment for many of those surveyed. In fact, almost 80% of the women surveyed chose one of these five traits as the childlike trait that helped make them successful.

Unlike the traits of the Warrior, where all five are critical for balance, you can be selective with the Little Girl traits. What gives you life, inspiration, freedom and fun will depend on you and what personally works for you.

Much like the Warrior exercises in the earlier chapters, we will delve further into each of the Little Girl traits and work on building them into your toolbox for everyday use. Do you remember your values work from Chapter 1? What values do you hold that help support these Little Girl traits? For instance, does your value of 'learning' help support your curiosity?

Curiosity
Excitement
Humor
Play
Possibility

Curiosity is wonder. It is what's beyond the obvious. You must have the desire to be curious or you can not authentically reap its benefits. Do you desire to meet new people and discover new things? Do you want to know more about the company you work for and how it operates within your industry?

There is always something new to learn, even in

things you already think you know. It's taking another perspective. It's seeing what's in front of you and assuming it isn't the answer; it's simply another clue. It's wanting to know more, see more, ask more.

Curiosity is also the cornerstone for creativity. If your Little Girl is not curious, you learn nothing new; and therefore, can not create anything new. Curiosity will not kill us. The unlucky cat was simply careless!

MELISSA

Melissa has an insatiable curiosity. As a Director for a Financial Services organization, she learns many new things by constantly asking questions and being willing to admit when she doesn't know something. She also does a lot of reading and researching of topics on her own. She has had excellent business success and her curiosity has served her well. The outcome from knowing all this new information and 'the big picture' is that she has been able to create a number of positions for herself. "Curiosity made me aware of many existing issues in the organization and I was then able to recognize what might be the next set of issues."

Curiosity starts from admitting that you don't know something and then desiring to know it. It builds knowledge and helps make work more interesting. As Writer Dorothy Parker once said "the cure for boredom is curiosity." Luckily, there is no cure for curiosity!

Many of us remember the adventures of Curious

George that kept us entertained for hours as children. Houghton Mifflin describes their most famous monkey like this. "For over sixty years, one little monkey has led the way into a world where delight and learning, friendship and excitement, come together in the joy of curiosity." It can be that way for you too.

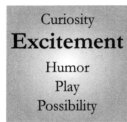

Curiosity
Excitement
Humor
Play
Possibility

I have heard over and over again, "I'm just not the type to show excitement." What does that mean? Is there only one way to be excited? Is it necessary to run through the halls of the company shouting out how happy you are to be working there? I think not. Excitement is personal and how you show it is personal as well. It can be just as powerful on the inside as for those who show it outwardly.

AMY

Amy, a vice-president for a non-profit, sees excitement as her best childlike quality. The excitement lives inside and out as she is known to get outwardly excited at a successful event or an unexpected donation. This trait not only works well for her, but also for those around her. It creates energy, motivation, and people get a kick out of seeing Amy's excitement.

TERRI

Terri has an unbridled enthusiasm. "I always try to see the positive and bring lots of enthusiasm to projects and general work life. I love being a group 'champion' and cheering on the 'team'. It keeps things fun and light-and others enjoy poking good-natured fun at my enthusiasm and idealism." This hasn't limited Terri's career growth. At the time of this interview, she was a vice-president of an international insurance company, making a six-figure salary.

There can however be a possible downside to strong enthusiasm. Over time Terri found herself fre-quently disappointed by others who were not as intense as she. "It led to struggles with colleagues and staff who were effective at their jobs but were not wired like me," she recalled. Terri has since left, like many other women, to start her own company. She didn't have to run however. It was possible to have this excitement and not reduce it to disappointment.

What Terri was missing was a strong Warrior to protect this wonderful Little Girl strength. Greater self-awareness would have provided her the understanding that she was blessed to feel such excitement in her daily work life, and that colleagues may not choose to follow that same path. This Warrior trait in combination with strength, would have allowed her to display her excite-ment with grace and not make others wrong. To realize that including the Little Girl traits in your life is a choice

114

and others get to not choose them, frees you from resentment. The righteousness of thinking everyone should be like you, takes away the amazing gifts you receive by having enthusiasm in your life. It makes it a requirement you expect from others.

Terri learned this after she left but doesn't regret the journey. "I never have regretted the enthusiasm and intensity I bring to my work. It's who I am and I can't be any other way. The error I made was thinking that others HAD to be the same way or that meant they didn't care, or weren't as competent and dedicated as me."

Your excitement not only adds value to your life, it is useful in motivating others to produce the best work possible. Just don't require that everyone else around you needs to show their enthusiasm the same way. And, it doesn't mean they aren't dedicated. People are different and show emotion differently even when feeling the same way.

Excitement is a reward for a job well done or the passion that comes with a deep connection to the work you do. Great moments in your life should not be taken for granted. It's hard to get excited when what you reap is expected. Good fortune is a gift, and don't we all love to get gifts?

> *"Only passions, great passions, can elevate the soul to great things"*
>
> *Denis Diderot French author & philosopher (1713 - 1784)*

Curiosity
Excitement
Humor
Play
Possibility

Over 30% of the women who participated in the survey chose humor as the Little Girl trait that worked well for them in their career. Humor relaxes those around you, diffuses situations and makes work a bit more fun. Being able to laugh at yourself eases stress and shows others you are human. It also helps you not to take yourself too seriously.

> *"A sense of humor is part of the art of leadership, of getting along with people, of getting things done."*
> Dwight D. Eisenhower, US General & Republican politician

SAMANTHA

Samantha is the highest ranking woman in a national healthcare organization and the only one on an all-male senior team. As CFO, she is responsible for several hundred employees and many strategic decisions. She believes humor has always been an important part of her being and has helped in her Senior Management role.

"Humor is great when something difficult needs to be said", says Samantha. "You can make a point in a light way. It also helps to be a bit self-deprecating. That diffuses many situations." Samantha has successfully held her executive job for over eight years, yet hasn't forgotten this positive Little Girl attribute.

Humor is not being the life of the party. In fact, notice what happens when someone tries too hard to be funny; they usually bomb. "Humor is tougher for women" says Cara, an officer in a financial services company. "We just can't get away with it so easily."
Obviously not all women feel this way. 30% of the women surveyed chose humor as their number one trait. While men may have an easier time of getting up, telling a joke or two and building relationships through humor, women have the same opportunity. They just have to be a bit more careful in how they use it.

NATALIE

Natalie, a non-profit executive, recalled to me a recent meeting where humor was especially helpful. This meeting consisted of many prominent leaders in her community, as well as executives from her organization–all men and for her, all intimidating. "They all wanted one decision, and I wanted the opposite. So, I was just 'myself' and joked about my choice being better than their choice for no better reason than because I wanted it. I said it with a good chuckle. It worked!"

Natalie's humor disarmed the situation. This allowed the others to be less serious and open their minds and ears to her idea. She, of course, still needed to sell it, but she had primed the pump with humor and it worked like a charm. By the end of the meeting, they had all changed their minds and agreed on her proposal.

LAUGHING AROUND THE GLOBE

There is a popular trend in India called The Laughter Club. Club members gather together regularly, and laugh. This fast-growing concept, originated by Dr. Mada Kararia, a Bombay physician, has over 25,000 members and 400 clubs. According to Michael Kerr, a certified Laughter Leader, "72% of laughter club members report improved interpersonal relationships with co-workers, 85% say it has improved their self-confidence and 66% suggest it has improved concentration."

A WORD OF CAUTION

There is a distinction between humor and humor at the expense of others. To go down the second that path, the Warrior trait of integrity is missing. As Jane Austin wrote in Emma, "Silly things do cease to be silly if they are done by sensible people in an impudent way."

What does seem to work for many of the women in the survey, is humor at their own expense. The anonymous quote of "Blessed are they who can laugh at themselves, for they will never cease to be amused" says it best. And, to be able to laugh at yourself is a powerful position.

Curiosity
Excitement
Humor
Play
Possibility

Somewhere along the way it became agreed upon that work wasn't supposed to be fun. And, although many companies have fun listed as a value in their mission statements, few have incorporated or integrated play into the daily work routine.

If you go to the park and watch children playing, it is much more than fun. Last year I was in Central Park on a beautiful summer day and I was watching the children on the swings. As they ran to them, they were making choices. One child ran around the swing set before choosing the swing she wanted. A little boy ran to a particular swing he noticed on his approach. Another child found a swing and instead of sitting on it immediately, stood on it first. They were playing but also making significant choices on what their 'fun' would look like.

Children playing on a see-saw is also an amazing thing to watch. It is masquerading as play but it's really more than that. You can only go as high as the person on the other end of the see-saw wants you to go. It really only works, and is fun, if both children work as hard as each other.

It seems like just play. However, incorporated in the play is partnership, evaluation, teamwork and choice. These are great lessons for business.

JULIE

Julie is an instructional designer, someone who designs educational courses for organizations. Play is an important part of her work. "I find that people engage in and apply learning more readily when it's fun and entertaining. With all the meetings that I attend, it's probably rare for me (and many others) to sit through a meeting without laughing with others, or at least chuckling to myself." For Julie, play not only helps people learn, it also encourages the Little Girl trait of humor.

DAWN

Dawn, a psychotherapist for many years, finds that incorporating playfulness puts others at ease and reduces tension. I asked her how she can utilize playfulness in her field and still remain credible. "I think my playfulness comes out in my humor. Sometimes I can twist a difficult or charged situation by pointing out with my humor, a different view of it. I have established myself as a credible therapist over the years which I think helps other people 'get' where I'm coming from."

Play increases learning, creates humor, reduces tension and much more. Don't put play at the bottom of your list. You could be losing a valuable partner in the enhancement of your work life.

Curiosity
Excitement
Humor
Play
Possibility

Remember Anita Roddick's comment about entrepreneurs? They "have pathological optimism. They never see a problem." This absolute optimism was clearly present with those individuals who saw the future possibility of starting a beauty business, a low-cost airline, an overnight delivery service or a home computer company.

Without a doubt, possibility and optimism were present when someone wondered if people would want to buy natural beauty products from a store, would wait in line for an assigned seat if it meant they would pay less for their flight, would pay $12 to get a package overnight or would want a computer in their home. When possibility is not present, opportunities are not presented.

In 1977 the president of Digital Equipment Company said, "There's no reason people would want computers in their homes." The possibility was not acknowledged and today there is no more Digital. There are many stories like this that are recounted in order to encourage open minds and optimistic attitudes. Without possibility, nothing more than the obvious would occur.

MYRA

Myra has had success in her career. As an assistant vice-president for a large financial services company, she enjoys credibility and respect. She has an incredibly strong external Warrior. That is what she chose to show and that is how she has experienced her work. Her Warrior attributes of integrity, courage, self-management and strength have served her well over the years. However by overly supporting all of her Warrior traits, she had buried her Little Girl qualities.

She came to me one summer because she was unhappy. She had been with the same company for some time and now felt unchallenged in her current position. She knew there was something different she wanted to do but didn't know what that might be.

We began to work together to envision what a great opportunity would look like. What was she curious about? What other areas within the company could she make a difference? What excites her about that thought? What possibilities currently exist in that area?

I asked her what it might be like if it were fun. "Fun? I had forgotten that work was once fun," she said.

We discussed her values of learning something new, making a difference, having a challenge. She talked about the love of communication and with all the changes at the company, she felt she could make a difference for the organization in this area. Off she went to begin looking into that possibility.

Later that fall an email landed in my box. "You transformed my life. Let's have lunch." This was intriguing and to tell the truth, quite satisfying. I couldn't wait to hear.

Myra had spent the summer reading and studying about change management and communication. She formulated a detailed proposal for the organization to consider and implement. Her ideas and plan were well received and she is now serving on an elite committee to help work on the organization's communication issues. Sitting before me at the Chinese lunch was a smiling, excited, outwardly enthusiastic Little Girl who had a renewed sense of possibility for her future.

REALIST OR PESSIMIST?

Many people justify the lack of openness to possibility as being a 'realist'. The difference between realism and pessimism is slight. Few things are not possible. Success often depends on what you're willing to do to achieve it. For many of us, from the time of our first disappointment as children, we're taught to get our heads out of the clouds. It's our parents' attempt at keeping us safe from disappointment. What it so often does is keep us from achieving anything more than what's safe. It's better to have believed and not achieved than never to have believed at all. For it most surely is true, you will not get what you haven't tried for.

Is some of your 'realism' really 'pessimism'? Build your Warrior's courage and take some chances.

Chapter Twelve

Accessing Your Little Girl

Accessing your Little Girl can be done with the same visioning exercise used in the Accessing your Warrior section of the book. There are however some important changes to what you are envisioning.

VISIONING

1) First of all, get comfortable. Find a place where you won't be disturbed and isn't noisy. You can be seated, laying down or standing if that works. Choose your position based on who you are.

2) Once you are in position, close your eyes and take some deep breaths. Slowly breathe in and out. Concentrate on that breath. Feel the air going into your nostrils, hold it, and let it out slowly through your mouth.

   With each breath, your body is relaxing. First your Toes. Then your knees. Breathe. Now your thighs. Breathe. Your stomach. Your chest. Breathe. Your arms and shoulders. Your neck. Your eyes. Breathe.

124

3) As you become more and more relaxed, picture yourself as a Little Girl. You are playing a game of some sort. What game is it? Was it a game you played as a child? Are you alone or is there someone else with you? Breathe. Just be with this for a minute or two. Embody your Little Girl. Feel her essence.

4) Now transport that being to a more familiar place; a place where you would be able to be this Little Girl. Where are you? What are the surroundings? What colors, sounds, feelings are there? What are you wearing? How are you dressed? Are you alone or are there others? Breathe.

   Get as detailed as you can. What does your hair look like? What is your expression? How are you standing? Where are your arms? Your hands? Really take all of this in. What's going on inside? If you could say something, what would it be?

   If you were to give her a name, what would that name be if it isn't your own? Something that encompasses who she is for you. Say that name. What happens when you call her name? Breathe.

As you hold your Little Girl inside of you, imagine a glow forming around her. Wherever she goes, the glow follows. Feel the warmth of the glow. That is your Little Girl's glow.

5) Slowly come back to your room. Recount all that you have seen and felt. Think of her name. Remember what makes her feel excited and curious. What possibilities does she believe in? This is your Little Girl. Embrace her. Call her forth when you need or want her. She is inside of you ready to come out. All you need to do is ask. Breathe.

When you open your eyes, write down your Little Girl experience. Some questions to answer: What does your Little Girl look like? What is her name? Does she remind you of someone?

_____

_____

_____

_____

_____

_____

_____

_____

CONSCIOUS CREATION

Guess what? You don't have to only envision, you can reminisce. You were once a Little Girl. If visioning doesn't work for you, try investigating.

Ask your parents, siblings and other relatives to describe how you were as a Little Girl. What were you like? Who were your friends? What games did you play? What did you want to be when you grew up? What was special about you? Did you have any expressions? How did the five Little Girl traits show up for you when you were a Little Girl? *Write these thoughts down.*

_____

_____

_____

_____

_____

_____

_____

_____

_____

_____

_____

OBSERVATION

Go to the park and watch the children. What are they
doing? How do they play? Create? What do they finding
exciting? What is it about them that you envy? *Write
these thoughts down.*

_____

_____

_____

_____

_____

_____

_____

_____

_____

_____

_____

_____

_____

_____

_____

Chapter Thirteen

Building your Little Girl

CURIOSITY; EXCITEMENT; HUMOR; PLAY; POSSIBILITY

Unlike the Warrior where all traits working together is critical, all your Little Girl traits working together at one time would probably have you sent away to some quiet place.

Not only will you not use all of your Little Girl traits at the same time, you may only be comfortable incorporating only one or two of the characteristics into your life. Perhaps you don't think you have the ability to be funny at all, but showing excitement or incorporating play into your routine is appealing. As mentioned earlier, unlike the five Warrior traits, you don't have to encompass all of the Little Girl traits to have a fulfilling Little Girl. You can pick and choose those qualities that most fit with who you naturally are.

WHERE ARE YOU NOW?

Think of a time when your Little Girl came forward in a situation and it was successful. What were the circumstances? Why did it work?

_____

_____

_____

_____

_____

The five Little Girl attributes and their definitions are in the table below. Like the Warrior exercise, rate yourself on a scale of one to ten (one not present; ten always present). Get five other people to rate you as well.

Attribute	Definition	Self	1	2	3	4	5	Avg
Curiosity	The desire to investigate, learn and understand.							
Humor	The ability to laugh or appreciate something funny.							
Excitement	The feeling of lively and cheerful joy.							
Play	To occupy oneself in amusement.							
Possibility	This is belief in a future prospect or potential.							
	Average							

What do your numbers look like? Are there any surprises? Are there vast differences between your thoughts and what others say? Where do you want to focus your attention? What do you want your ultimate Little Girl to look like? *Write down your thoughts.*

_____

_____

_____

_____

_____

_____

_____

_____

WHERE ARE YOU GOING?

You now need to set your intentions. The chart on the next page serves as a pictorial of where you are headed. Remember, real life does not go as smoothly as it does on paper so don't get discouraged. This simply helps to focus you and give you direction. Again, journey, journey, journey.

Carry over your numbers from the last exercise and put them in the Now column. Then, just like the Warrior intentions chart, decide where it is you want to go. Unlike the Warrior, you may have some zeros for the qualities you don't want to incorporate into your life.

Little Girl Trait	Now	Future
Curiosity		
Humor		
Excitement		
Play		
Possibility		

You now know where you are and where you are going. Let's work the traits one by one with some helpful ways to strengthen each. Much like the Warrior work, review all of the areas. You may learn something new.

CURIOSITY

> "The important thing is not to stop questioning. Curiosity has its own reason for existing."
> Albert Einstein

Is it that we lose our childlike curiosity when we grow up or are we simply too afraid that others will think (or know) we don't know? For most, it's the latter. We just don't want to look bad.

Curiosity allows us to explore rather than accept what is going on around us. Curious people learn a lot and curiosity gives us the information we need to be success-ful.

The first thing to do is discover what happened to your curiosity and when you think you began to suppress it. Have you decided you know and understand everything? Have you equated asking questions with being stupid? *Write down your thoughts.*

_____

_____

_____

_____

_____

_____

ABBY

For Abby, a bank vice president, her sense of discovery and awe at learning new things and meeting new people has served her well in getting to the heart of important issues. This curiosity shows up as "interest, openness to others, and a safe space for others to be with me." Abby believes this is being, not doing. When she can stop what she's doing, and give herself time to think, she naturally feels a great sense of discovery.

When her curiosity doesn't seem present, she sits still, doesn't check email, and doesn't move around. She consciously stops doing anything and sits there so she can be open to her thoughts. If she's with others, she sits there and listens.

NICOLE

Nicole, a director in a non-profit organization, finds that her desire to learn leads her to ask questions and 'see the whole picture'. This curiosity has served her well over the years and a former mentor, when she was in the newspaper business, told her it made her a good reporter.

JESSICA

Jessica finds curiosity to be an asset in her position as a trainer at an international, blue-chip company. It has provided her a lot of knowledge for her to perform her job better. This trait however, is not viewed the same by everyone she works with. "Senior people usually respond well to my questions and simply answer them. My coworkers seem to have mixed reactions. Some admire me for having the guts to ask, as they want the answer too. Some are concerned that I might hurt myself (especially if it is a question that I should perhaps have known the answer to). And some (mostly the ones who don't say much in a meeting, but then express their opinions outside of the meeting) express dismay that I am delaying the meeting by asking questions! The last are few and far between, but they do exist." Remember to work on your Warrior's knowledge so you do know many of the answers you should, and remember timing is key.

The Warrior and The Little Girl

BUILDING YOUR CURIOSITY

1) Ask questions. When you think you've asked the last possible one, ask another.
2) Ask open-ended questions, not just ones that can be answered with a yes or no. Ask how/why?
3) Don't be attached to the answers. Keep an open mind.
4) Look beyond the obvious. What more is there?
5) Practice on strangers. Find out about their lives, where they are going, where they got that nice coat, etc. Make sure you let them go. We don't want you arrested for stalking.

EXCITEMENT

JULIA

Julia, an independent copywriter, believes excitement adds a lot to her work life. I asked her how she brings it forth. "Well, I look at Henry (her 3-year old son) and he sees the world with fresh eyes. Because of his age, he's not jaded...never just shrugs his shoulders and says 'been there, done that.' That's what I make a deliberate effort to do in my work. Every new assignment is a fresh chance to do something great."

Remaining excited about what you do for a living is a choice. You can allow yourself to get stale, or you can see each opportunity that comes your way as a new adventure. It is perspective. If you approach something as exciting, it will be exciting. Every new thing you take on is a chance to do something great. In fact, perhaps the best you've ever done. That's exciting!

DONNA

Donna is in the business of finance. This is traditionally looked at as a dull line of business. In order to make her work exciting, Donna views it as a mystery to be solved. It's a puzzle and the pieces need to fit together. This gets her wheels turning and her excitement flowing.

ALICE

Alice, a marketing executive for almost a decade, has many 'tricks' to keep her excitement high. She approaches all projects, (even if they've been done before) as new, giving it a new name. She introduces the project to her staff, with excitement, like they never did it before.

She also rotates responsibilities in order to maintain excitement, increase the possibility of new ideas, and ensure that the staff is well trained.

If it's a project she can do with her eyes closed, such as a report, she starts from the bottom up, creating the appearance of newness.

The bottom line is her commitment to having excitement in her work has evolved into a process of making it happen. Simply her awareness that she needs the value excitement, has supported her commitment. "I really do have it inside of me to inject excitement and energy in most things. I feel truly blessed to have this ability. It certainly helped my overall feelings about work because we all have control over how we view our work and I choose to be excited about what I do." Finding excitement in your everyday work rubs off positively on co-workers, improves quality and certainly makes the day fly by.

Choice is a critical word here. You can choose to look for excitement in your job or choose not to. Many women before you have recognized the value of this Little Girl energy in the work they do, whether internally or externally. As a managing director for an international consulting company, Iris finds that her excitement and energy encourages people to be around her. "It's also good when doing presentations, planning and facilitating meetings, etc. It makes people pay positive attention to you and helps engage them."

DINA

Dina, a recent graduate working in the financial services industry receives a lot of positive feedback for her excitement. "I know people around here notice my enthusiasm because I've gotten positive feedback from bosses. I think it's just a matter of being quick to help out and get things done. I think having a positive attitude and being personable also helps me to portray enthusiasm."

What happens when she forgets to bring this Little Girl quality to work? "I think it's just a matter of noticing when I'm feeling lazy and making myself get in front of people and asking for something new to work on. I think my enthusiasm has certainly helped me impress people I work for because they believe that I want to be here and I want to work, which will make them more and more inclined to give me greater responsibilities."

It's a choice. You do not have to be born with the 'excitement gene' in order to learn to be excited. Working on your Little Girl curiosity trait will help in building your commitment to excitement. The bottom line is that 18-months into her job for a very big financial services company, Dina made assistant vice president. Of course, it was more than her enthusiasm that got her the promotion. But perhaps it was that excitement that got her the attention.

JOAN

In order to have excitement, Joan, a human resource director, needs to be doing work that's in line with her values which allow her to be authentic and true to herself. "I am generally optimistic and look for the best in people. Making real connections and feeling I'm making a difference energizes me and it shows. Engaging with people and looking for their uniqueness keeps it fresh."

ADDING EXCITEMENT INTO YOUR WORK

1) Do a reality check. Name anything exciting about the work you do or the place you do it.
2) If it's not that exciting now, is it possible it could be in the future?
3) Observe others who show excitement. What does it look like? How do you know they are excited?
4) Take a challenge, learn something new, ask for a change in assignment, or go about your workday differently.
5) Establish a reward system for yourself that provides you incentive for certain achievements. I happen to get very excited and very motivated at the thought of a day at the spa or a night out with the ladies as a reward for a job well done.

HUMOR

Humor is a great thing, a saving thing. It is such an important part of life and well-being. The minute humor crops up, many of our irritations, resentments and negative attitudes slip away and a sunny spirit takes their place.

VALERIE

Valerie, an advertising vice-president, finds humor in everything. "You have to know the audience pretty well and listen to find the funny insight" she offers. "I took a year-long course in improvisational comedy when I lived in Chicago at the start of my career. I was in advertising and was having to make presentations and it terrified me. So I joined the Second City improv school. It was one of the best things I have ever done as it taught me to think on my feet and not be scared of being on stage."

TIMING

BARBARA

With humor, you also need timing. Barbara, a vice president in financial services, finds that because she believes that work should be fun, she is not taken seriously at times. In addition, at times when she is being serious, it is unsettling to those around her as they take it personally. "I am not being rude when serious, but it is perceived as so simply because it is not light hearted. I also feel that because of this strong personality trait, I have to work twice as hard to prove I am intelligent and competent. I've tried to be different but it doesn't really suit me. It's frustrating."

What Barbara needs is more balance of the Warrior and the Little Girl. She too often defers to her Little Girl in order to avoid conflict, to be liked, and to be 'easy' to be around. This does not serve her in other areas such as credibility and power.

APPROPRIATENESS

Knowing your audience is a very important aspect of humor, unless it's the person on the elevator and you won't see them again. Patty found this out the hard way when she was working with a colleague on a project and she forgot something. She explained to this colleague that she suffered 'an attack of early Alzheimer's.' Her colleague looked shocked and speechlessly walked away. Later Patty learned that her colleague's father-in-law was dying from Alzheimer's disease.

Some women also use humor to avoid taking responsibility for a mistake or to avoid conflict. This usually doesn't serve them well as they are not taken seriously. A strong Warrior's courage is necessary to balance the scales. The key to humor is to know when to use it and when not to. Remember to pay attention to your audience. You'll be able to tell fairly quickly if they appreciate your humor—or not.

PRACTICE

Humor, in reality, can't be forced. It's quite obvious when someone is trying to be funny, and quite painful when they're obviously not. But, lightness can be practiced and balance can be found.

1) Practice on strangers. Again, strangers are great. It doesn't matter what they think of you.

If they don't think you're funny, so what? Start a conversation in the elevator and keep it light. If something funny occurs to you, give it a go. You'll probably never see them again. You have little to lose.

2) Try to look for something funny in everything you come in contact with. Ask yourself, what's funny about that?

3) Read a book by a comedian. Something by Ellen Degeneres or Dave Barry always provides a good belly laugh.

4) Watch others who you think use humor well in business and occasionally integrate some of their approaches into your conversations.

5) Start with a warm smile. It's not that hard and it's recognized by almost anyone, in any language. It is disarming and welcoming. "It always seems to make things work when developing relationships with clients," says Mary, VP of Operations with a telecommunications company. Make it authentic though. False smiles are very obvious. And for Pete's sake, show some teeth!

Much like courage, humor can be built. It starts with opening yourself up to get connected to others, breaking down some barriers and being outside yourself.

CHRYSTINA

Chrystina is a smart, young new executive. Over educated for her experience, she takes herself very seriously. She has a limited sense of humor, even when those around her are laughing. Her Warrior is very strong and she wears her Warrior on her sleeve. Chrystina's integrity is obvious, her belief in social issues unending and her self-management strong. Actually too strong as she comes across guarded and makes those around her a bit uncomfortable. This hinders her relationship building. She needs to lighten up and allow herself to experience and enjoy what's funny in life, even when there are some unfunny things in the world.

Barbra Streisand, a Warrior extraordinaire, came out of 'retirement' to do *Meet the Fockers*. Here is a woman who is a strong political supporter, opposed to injustice of any kind and admired by many of her peers and her fans. She understands that even in a world where there is pain, we can, and must, still laugh. Humor doesn't mean other things aren't important.

Humor is an important part of life. It's freeing, it's healing and as human beings, we have a multitude of opportunities to laugh. "I like to look for the humor in everyday stuff. When people laugh together (even at work) it makes work more fun," offers Julie, a Director for a telecommunications firm in New York City.

PLAY/FUN

Play shows up in many different ways and fundamentally depends on who you are and the type of organization you are in. It doesn't necessarily mean playing is your number one focus, it could mean you are encouraging play in others. When you are present to play, you will undoubtedly reap benefits as well.

JUDY

For Judy, a corporate trainer for over 18 years, it's a natural part of the learning process. "My trademark is stress balls. I offer one to anybody who is already stressed or worried about what they are supposed to learn. During class, if someone gives a good answer, I will throw a ball to them. At the end of class, they return all the balls to me and then I throw one to one student to name 'one thing they learned today' and then they must throw it to another student and tell the class what they learned, etc. It gets people to relax, laugh and have fun-and they will remember better what they learned!"

SAMANTHA

Samantha, a vice-president in higher education, thinks of her work as her 'play time'. She tries to make work fun for her and for the people who work with her. "We should approach our work with energy and passion, the way kids approach playing a game or other pastimes that they really love," she offers. To encourage play, she injects brainstorming and creative activities into staff discussions when they are faced with a problem to solve.

> ## WHY PLAY?
> **5** great reasons
>
> 1) Keeps life fun.
> 2) It encourages curiosity.
> 3) Helps us relax and lighten up.
> 4) Breeds humor.
> 5) Helps build relationships and teams.

According to the Institute For Play, most Nobel Laureates, innovative entrepreneurs, artists and performers, well-adjusted children and many more, play enthusiastically throughout their lives. The Institute offers, "What common denominator is shared by mass murderers, abused children, burnt-out employees, depressed mothers, caged animals and chronically worried students? Play is rarely or never a part of their lives."

LAUREN

We all define play differently and what play looks like to you is critical. Lauren, a high-ranking lobbyist in Washington finds that play is critical to her work and a real asset. Here is a page from her playlist.

1) Enjoying a non-work related function or event with someone you work with.
2) Learning that someone you work with on Capitol Hill loves to play golf and taking the time to play a round.
3) Introducing a fellow worker/government colleague to a new restaurant.
4) Organizing a group of women lobbyists and Congressional staffers to visit a Washington Museum and have lunch afterwards.
5) Talking to a group of Grade/High School students about energy.
6) Incorporating a non-profit function (community activism, volunteer reader, shelter) into the daily profit routine.

The list, as well as her optimism and energy, is endless. She sees all of this as play and reaps many of the same rewards as Samantha or Judy. Plus, there is some very powerful networking going on at the same time.

INCORPORATE PLAY INTO YOUR WORK

1) Investigate the ways you like to play.
2) What hobbies can you incorporate into your work? Take up a hobby if you don't have one. Make it something much different than what you do on a day-to-day basis. If you're not comfortable playing during the workday,

schedule play in your free time and reap the benefits at work.

3) Investigate ways you could motivate your staff through play.

4) Do something totally different. Take a different route to work. Take the stairs and not the elevator. Go out to lunch instead of eating at your desk.

5) Invite the 'girls' from the office out for dinner, a movie, or a great concert.

POSSIBILITY

Where others say 'no way,' Peggy says 'yes, it can be done'. Anything is possible for her. This is her choice and, for her, it's an important choice to make. Her life would be incomplete without possibility.

There's a great story whose source is unknown, although motivational speaker and business consultant Stephen Covey has been known to tell it. It takes place during a time management course. The instructor held up a big jar and placed enough large rocks in it so no more would fit. He asked the attendees if the jar was full. Most said yes.

He then reached under the table and pulled out a box with some small rocks and proceeded to put those rocks into the jar until no more of them would fit. Again he asked if the jar was full. Only a few people said yes.

He then pulled out a bag containing sand and poured the sand into the jar until no more sand would fit. Again he asked if the jar was full. No one said yes.

He then took a pitcher of water and filled the jar until it couldn't take any more. He then asked if anyone could tell him the lesson. No one could.

The lesson was that you must put the big things in your life first. The smaller things will find a way in on their own. But, if you don't put in the big things first, they won't fit in later.

This is a great story for time management, but it's even a better story for possibility. When the jar was filled with big rocks, adding more looked impossible. But it was possible. Not only once, but three more times. You just have to ask "What else?"

INCORPORATE POSSIBILITY INTO YOUR WORK

1) Post the words "What Else?" where you can see them. This will remind you to go beyond the obvious.
2) Ask yourself, "what are the next steps possible for me in my career?"
3) Take time to dream of what's possible. Get really crazy, you won't hurt yourself.
4) Ask yourself, "if there wasn't anything in the way, what would be possible?"
5) If it is possible, are you willing to do the work?

The Warrior and The Little Girl

CURIOSITY; EXCITEMENT; HUMOR; PLAY; POSSIBILITY

80% of those surveyed picked one of these five as a characteristic that helped bring them success. Perhaps it's time you picked one too.

Nice girls may not get the corner office according to Lois P. Frankel, Ph.D., Good girls may not get ahead according to Kate White, editor-in-chief of Redbook. However there is a successful and fulfilling place for these key Little Girl attributes. As Picasso once said "Every child is an artist. The problem is how to remain an artist once he grows up."

Where are you now?

You may have come back down to mind-ful with bad results. That's normal. You're learning new things.

Unmindful with good results

Mindful with good results

Mindful with bad results

Unmindful with bad results

149

Chapter Fourteen

Calling up your Little Girl

Until your Little Girl becomes a natural integration into your life, it's important to develop a way that you can call her forth. There are a number of ways you can summon her at the right times.

SOMETHING TO SEE

Whether it's a picture of you that reminds you of your Little Girl self or an object or toy you had as a child you, something visual is very helpful. Think for a moment what object you can identify that reminds you of your Little Girl qualities. When you have that item, put it in a place that is easily accessible. I carry a picture of myself at about five in my wallet.

In addition, you can post the Little Girl traits in a place that you will see on a daily basis. This serves as a reminder of all the tools available to you. I have mine posted on the cabinet door above the computer monitor.

SOMETHING TO DO

Unlike the Warrior traits where forms of breathing, walking, meditation or yoga poses are helpful, calling up your Little Girl requires a bit more energy. Play, humor and excitement are not usually quiet activities. There are a number of ways to get inspired.

I find it helpful to occasionally visit a park and watch the children play. There are so many lessons to be learned. Spend some time relaxing in the park, swing on the swings, get in touch with the child within.

Whenever my son asks me a question I don't know the answer to, we look it up together on the internet. For instance, we both find out why the sky is blue, why it rains and what makes it thunder. While I don't use this information daily, the search awakens me to ask other questions that may be more pertinent.

Your Little Girl will be a source of energy in your life. She will become an integral part of who you are, but remember, timing is critical. Because there is sometimes danger in showing your Little Girl at inappropriate or unsafe times, you'll need to get really good at evaluating appropriateness. Here are some questions you can ask yourself to evaluate whether it's safe or appropriate for your Little Girl to come to tea.

1) Review your organization's culture. Is there any excitement, play, humor? Do people ask questions easily? Is out-of-the-box thinking rewarded?

2) Do you have good common sense? Can you read situations quickly and easily? This helps determine if it's suitable for your Little Girl to show up.

3) Do you tend to go too far? Remember, over the top excitement, inappropriate humor and play when you should be serious are hard to recover from. You'll need to make sure your self-management attribute is in full force.

4) Do you have a credibility issue? If you do, you may want to concentrate on your Warrior traits first and build that credibility. Little Girl qualities are more appreciated and welcomed from a credible source.

5) And for the record, it is never appropriate to dress like a Little Girl.

While needing extra care than your Warrior, your Little Girl has so much to offer you. Take the time to cultivate her marvelous qualities carefully, in a way that will bring joy, fun and energy into your daily work.

---

5 Little Girl Check Points

1) Review your culture.
2) Check your common sense.
3) Know your limits.
4) Know your credibility issues.
5) Dress for success.

Chapter Fifteen

Little Girl Confusion

The 75 women in the survey were asked what trait didn't work for them in their careers. Very few chose the stereotypical traits of "niceness", "compassion" and "nurturing". In fact, the same percentage of women who chose these as challenging traits, chose them as traits that helped them get ahead.

Over half, 58%, gave childlike qualities such as defensiveness, impatience, shyness and show of emotion as examples. These are all real traits. You are human and not perfect. There are however powerful Warrior ways that can be very helpful when your less than optimal Little Girl traits come to visit.

DEFENSIVENESS

I once worked for a company where the culture was one of 'aggressively giving negative feedback.' This of course brought out my Little Girl in the form of defensiveness. I was very sure, based on my historical information of myself, that if I had been approached differently, I would have been able to take it much better. Not perfectly. I admit I have a defensive side.

Unfortunately, the world is full of people who don't

know how to communicate effectively in order to produce the best results in others. That's what keeps me busy in my communication coaching and consulting business.

That being said, I gained the reputation of being sometimes defensive. Once this started, it was very difficult to change this perception.

Defensiveness is wide-spread and not limited to younger, inexperienced women. For CEO Rose, it shows up "when I feel threatened, over my head, or unappreciated. If other people are asked for information or advice about what I'm most qualified at, and my opinion is not asked, or taken, I get defensive."

There are three Warrior traits that can be very helpful here. Knowledge ensures you are well informed about your job, and limits how threatened you feel. This will build the confidence you need to reduce the fear that is causing the defensive behavior. Self-management will help you take some breaths and pause, so that you don't make a knee-jerk comment you'll regret later.

Lastly, you can use your integrity/honesty quality to coach those around you to communicate differently if they are attacking. Pick and choose whom to do this with based on where you feel safe by saying something like, "I appreciate your feedback. Could we find a more constructive way to communicate so that we work better as a team?"

Believe it or not, there is a very effective Little Girl trait that can help overcome defensiveness as well. It's curiosity. Donna, an international independent consultant finds her curiosity very helpful. "A client recently gave me some feedback saying, 'you need to be running the show more and have a more structured agenda.' My immediate internal, emotional reaction was 'I sent you a very structured agenda already, with 4-5 agenda items. How is this not structure and not running the show?' Instead, I took a deep breath and asked 'What does my agenda need to look like in order for it to be more structured for you?' And then he gave me a very detailed answer which was perfect - because he designed me to be exactly what he needed. My curiosity along with suspending judgment for just long enough to not react defensively allowed the situation to be absolutely ideal for both of us. Now he's happy I'm doing the structured thing, and I know exactly what he needs."

SULKING

Let's continue my story for a minute. So, I would be attacked, get defensive, be attacked more, and then shut down; my own form of sulking. Not very professional but humanly necessary as my flight or fight reflexes were stimulated and fighting wasn't appropriate. So, I flew, yet still stayed in the room. This unfortunately accomplished two things: 1) made me look like a child and 2) allowed my aggressors to win as I left my power on the table.

While these reactions were created for protection, they are my demons. However, once I recognized that these were reactions to people's aggressiveness toward me, I started to see my Little Girl reactions coming before they did. To protect myself, I call upon my Warrior to help me stand tall. I breathe. I think. I smile. I comment calmly; whatever it takes to not fall into the wounded Little Girl.

Take a moment to think about your demons. What are they? How do they show up? Where don't they serve you well?

_____

_____

_____

_____

Once you have them listed, think about some ways you could derail them. Here are some ideas:

1) Breathe.
2) Silently say hello and thank them for coming to the rescue. However, ask them to be silent as you assess the situation.
3) If you're in a meeting, begin writing things down. Anything which puts the focus on the information coming at you and not what is getting stirred up in your body.
4) Ask your aggressor to explain what they mean in more detail, more clearly or another way. Get curious.
5) If asked for your response, let them know you need some time to address the situation.

IMPATIENCE

17% of the women surveyed said that impatience was a quality that didn't work for them. This showed up in a number of ways including not delegating and losing tempers. For Alice it sacrifices her relationships with her staff. "When I want something done and I think that the other person will not get it done fast enough, I will do it myself or at least start the project myself. This is not exactly team playing. It's not that I think I can do it better (well, sometimes!), it's that I hate to be late with anything and it comes down to control."

Patience shows up in the Warrior traits of inner and outer strength, as well as self-management. Leonardo da Vinci had one of the most wonderful thoughts about patience. "Patience serves as a protection against wrongs as clothes do against cold. For if you put on more clothes as the cold increases, it will have no power to hurt you. So in like manner you must grow in patience when you meet with great wrongs, and they will then be powerless to vex your mind." As you build your Warrior, so too will you build your patience.

A word of caution. Too much patience could indicate a lack of urgency or a presence of fear. It's a balance. Patience has its limits.

SHYNESS

Several women indicated that shyness was a trait that

didn't work for them. It limited their advancement, hurt their relationships, and took away their power. No one indicated it was a positive quality. And, it certainly isn't one of the five effective Little Girl traits.

Cara is a competent and shy person. Her work is exemplary, her commitment unmatched, and her capabilities unequaled at her executive level. Overcoming her shyness to get her job done effectively is exhausting. "High-energy people exhaust me. I have to pump myself up to 'be' present in these situations. I need to picture my Warrior at these times."

The Little Girl trait of curiosity will help greatly to combat your shyness. Get curious with the people you are speaking with. People love to talk about themselves. Asking questions means you don't have to provide so much of the conversation.

WHINING

There is a distinction between the Warrior's quest for justice and the Little Girl's whining. The feelings and the goals may be the same, but the delivery is the key.

I was brought in as a consultant for a company to handle a major marketing and communications project over an extended period of time. The client was already behind schedule when I arrived so they brought someone of my level in to hit the ground running in order to catch up. Needless to say, I was knee deep in creative, planning, scheduling and relationship building from day one. By my third week, a senior copywriter went to her bosses' boss (the woman I worked directly with) and with a quivering lower lip, announced I was not nice to her.

When this was brought to my attention, I immediately wondered what I had done. It's where we immediately go. I had three encounters with her over the three weeks. The first was during a meeting together where I told her I had a good friend who was also a copywriter and that I could hook her up with my friend for partnering if she'd like; the second was a brainstorming session and the third was a request from me for some information on a name she suggested for a new product.

Here's the point. Let's say during one of these three meetings I was a little short. If she had a developed Warrior, she would have had the courage to come to me, sit down and ask, "Did we get off on the wrong foot?" "Is there a different way of working together that would be more effective?" "When you abruptly asked for more information, it was bothersome to me."

There is no integrity in whining. In fact, it takes away all of your credibility. I know. At times I am a whiner. I don't mean to be but sometimes my frustration comes out in tones that are no doubt, whines. It's interesting that during the first conversation about this woman's complaint, I used my Warrior's strength by replying, "What specifically did I do so I can clean it up with her?" "I'll handle this however you would like in order for us to move forward." Unfortunately, the second time it was mentioned, I responded by whining. "Why didn't she just come to me? This is ridiculous. We have work to do." Those comments by themselves sound fine, but the tone was no doubt, a whine. This lessened my credibility. My Warrior's strength was overcome by my childlike confusion. Not a good approach for business.

To change whining to Warrior you need to approach topics more powerfully. 1) topic (choose wisely), 2) tone (clearly and without emotion, make your statement), and 3) words (ask for something you need, don't just complain).

Ask yourself:

1) What is it that isn't working for me?
2) Is this something I should bring up or could it be an isolated instance?
3) Who would be the best person to talk to? (Think of the politics, the openness of the person you choose.)
4) What would be the best approach in tone and language?
5) What is it I need to have different in this situation in order to make it work? What am I willing to do, or alter in order to make the situation better?

EXCESSIVE VULNERABILITY

Vulnerability is not necessarily a bad thing. We are all vulnerable at times, yet many women use this to their detriment. Sue, a very smart, capable marketing executive believes her vulnerability has worked well for her. She is petite, quiet and cute, and she looks younger than she is. Her outward appearance is one of vulnerability. This has worked well as many men (and some women) in the workplace seem to go out of their way to treat her nicely.

While she may get what she needs most of the time, this also limits her power and authority by way she is perceived. Too much vulnerability is considered a weakness in business. When the going gets tough, as it always does at some stage in the business cycle, they'll go get someone else. Consequently for Sue, she's reached the highest level she can in her organization. The fact is she is not perceived powerful enough for the next management position. Fortunately for Sue, she seems okay and she's reasonably happy where she is. Therefore, her use of vulnerability serves her well. If she had wanted to go higher in the organization, she would need her Warrior to help her overcome her outward vulnerability. These are the choices we make.

BEING TOO NICE

A few women indicated that the trait that didn't work for them was being too nice. In itself, there is nothing wrong with being nice. It's a wonderful way of being and does not make you weak. What you let happen to you because of your niceness is what doesn't work.

Rachael works for an international consulting company, as a senior member of the team. "Being too nice hasn't worked well for me. In a work environment, people tend to take advantage of you." The truth is, they don't take advantage of you because you're nice, they take advantage of you because you let them. The Warrior qualities of courage, integrity and honesty would work well here. Have the courage to say what you really feel and clearly say 'No!' The question for Rachael is "What fear is stopping you from saying no?" The trait that doesn't work is wanting to be liked at all costs, not being nice. There is nothing wrong with being kind, friendly and nice.

The Warrior as your Partner

Every woman surveyed indicated a trait that didn't work for them. Over half had something to do with the seven discussed above. The good news is, your Warrior can be a valuable partner in your quest to manage the confused Little Girl traits that don't serve you well. On the next page is a chart with each of the seven Little Girl Confusion traits and the Warrior traits that can help.

Confusion Trait	Warrior Counterpart
Defensiveness	Self-management; Honesty
Sulking	Self-management, Courage
Impatience	Inner/Outer Strength
Shyness	Honesty; Self-management; Courage
Whining	Self-management; Integrity; Courage
Excessive Vulnerability	Courage; Inner/Outer Strength
Too Nice	Courage; Integrity; Honesty

A WORD ABOUT PRESENTATIONS

While not a point of Little Girl confusion, presentations suffer from not knowing how to balance power and personality. For some of my career I made the mistake of inviting only my Warrior to presentations I would make. While I would do a fine job, very little of my personality came through. If I do say so myself, I am naturally funny (although some of my friends disagree!), sincere, full of excitement and believe in endless possibility. Picture a presentation where all the material was correct, I was strong in my presentation, and the audience left well informed. That's not bad, but there was a lost opportunity. They did not get to experience the information the same way I experienced it, only how I delivered it. They left informed but dispassionate. This made me think about the presentation skills of the managers in my own group and one day I decided to raise the bar.

I brought in a presentation coach for a half day because we had an important sales meeting coming up and I wanted us to get additional coaching. I joined the managers in this workshop. I had always gotten feedback that I was a good presenter. All the pieces were there but there was something missing. After my run through, the coach immediately said to me, "What are you holding back? Your personality is much bigger." This brought out my real concern of too much of my Little Girl coming across and losing my credibility. I was always concerned that I would be taken differently than I had intended. In the process, I had purposely uninvited my Little Girl qualities to my presentations and therefore left them lacking in excitement.

The coach instructed me to do the presentation again with all of my personality. He needed to see what I was talking about. I did it again in front of him and my staff, and they loved it. They didn't think I was over the top. They thought I was effective, informative, energizing, powerful and fun. I have never left my Little Girl out since and I have really become much better at presenting.

Be careful with your Little Girl however. Too much may reduce your credibility. Susan, a Chief of Staff for a top insurance company, has been told that her style of communicating (which is to 'connect' with her audience in a personal way) gives the impression that she lacks confidence. "That I am too concerned about what the audience will think and how they are receiving my message versus simply delivering my 'cut and dry' information. At one point in my career, this was a key reason for not being offered a new position."

Susan is stuck in the black and white of either being forceful with her information or giving too much power to her audience. This can be a problem for women speakers. Checking in with the audience is fine, but asking permission to take a certain path or asking too many times if there is understanding, reduces credibility greatly. The Warrior trait of outer strength will help alleviate this tendency. In public speaking, lead with your Warrior and bit by bit, gain the confidence and poise to summon your Little Girl along the way.

Chapter Sixteen

The Journey
is Just Beginning

While you may think this is the end of your journey, I can assure you, it is really just the beginning. The combined ten traits of the Warrior and the Little Girl might at first glance appear to be easily integrated into your life, however, you will need to work to have them at the core of your being. If you did all the exercises along the way, you worked hard. Putting it into practice however is the ultimate challenge. And, in the beginning, most of your learning will be retrospective. That means you'll mess up and realize it later. The good news is, you may not mess up the next time, or the time after that.

Being able to summon up all ten will not mean you are perfect. It will mean you now have the ability to effectively use them. The fact is, no one is perfect. We all mess up somewhere along the way. After all of this work and all this time, I sometimes still get defensive. I show my emotion, or I do or say something inappropriate. Here's the difference. I am very clear about myself, my motives and my competence. I am good at many things, not so good at others. I have learned how to separate them so that I don't put everything I'm about in one basket so that when I do trip up, it isn't overwhelming.

A final word of advice. Whenever you are going into a new environment, lead with your Warrior. Until you know what is acceptable and what the atmosphere is like, your Little Girl is not safe. It's always wise to have your Warrior present, in some capacity, at all times. Knowing when to lead with one or the other is where the real knowledge and power lies.

CHARTING YOUR COURSE

It is time to set up your Warrior and Little Girl work plan. How will you approach your journey? What will you concentrate on? Where will you get assistance? A simple chart will help you focus. There is a sample of the beginnings of one at the end of this chapter.

Each of the ten traits (all five Warrior and all five Little Girl) should have a box. That is so all ten are always present and top of mind. Remember, you need to have all five Warrior traits present to be a full Warrior. You can pick the Little Girl traits that will serve you best. Make your plan, set your goals, and get yourself started.

Remember, you're not searching for perfection.

So I'm in a yoga class the other day and I need to find my "Drishdi." Drishdi is your focus, where you're thinking about nothing at all but being. I'm in the dancer's pose (standing on one leg, the other leg behind me being held by the same side hand, and my other hand in front of me) and I'm thinking, 'where's my drishdi, where's my drishdi?' Then I think 'stop thinking where your drishdi is, you're not supposed to be thinking.' That was the last thing that went through my mind before I lost my balance and hit the floor. It's always searching for perfection and not staying present in the moment that gets us off balance.

Remember the ladder? Depending upon how hard you worked while reading the book, you are somewhere between Mindful with Bad Results and Mindful with Good Results. Wherever you are, you are now more powerful than when you first opened this book.

You are now aware of what's possible and what you are missing. Keep going. The stakes are high, and the rewards are even greater.

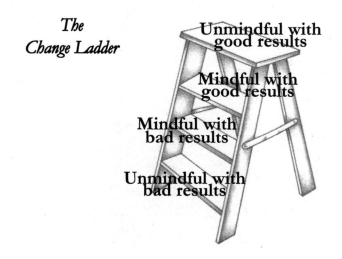

The
Change Ladder

Unmindful with good results

Mindful with good results

Mindful with bad results

Unmindful with bad results

A SAMPLE PORTION OF A WARRIOR AND LITTLE GIRL WORK PLAN.

Characteristic	Item	By When
Courage	Make a list of courageous things to do.	6/15/05
	Narrow the list to three and prioritize.	6/30/05
	Begin to do support work for the first courageous move (read a book on salary negotiation, network with people in the field, etc).	7/1/05
Humor	Read a book on humor in the workplace.	6/30/05
	Begin to smile more with co-workers and at more strangers.	immediately

Resources

Self Awareness

<u>Stand up for your Life</u>, Cheryl Richardson, Free Press, 2002.

<u>The New Agreements in the Workplace</u>, David Dibble, Emeritis Group & The New Dream Team, 2002.

<u>Wherever you go, There you are</u>, Jon Kabat-Zinn, Hyperion, 1994.

<u>The Right Questions</u>, Debbie Ford, HarperSanFrancisco, 2003.

<u>Transitions: Positive Change in Your Life and Work</u>, Barrie Hopson & Mike Scally, Pfeiffer and company, 1988

<u>The Seven Spiritual Laws of Success</u>, Deepak Chopra, Amber-Allen Publishing and New World Library, 1993.

<u>The Road Less Traveled</u>, M. Scott Peck, M.D., Simon & Schuster, 1978.

<u>Finding your own North Star</u>, Martha Beck, Three Rivers Press, 2001.

<u>Wishcraft: How to get what you really want</u>, Barbara Sher & Annie Gottlieb, 2003.

Warrior

The Warrior Within, John Little, Contemporary Books, 1996.

The Four-Fold Way, Angeles Arrien, PhD., HarperSanFrancisco, 1993.

The 100 Most Influential Women of All Time, Deborah G. Felder, Kensington Publishing Corp., 2001

Women Who Run with the Wolves, Clarissa Pinkola Estes, Ballantine Books, 1996.

Play Like a Man, Win Like a Woman, Gail Evans, Broadway Books, 2000.

Little Girl

Think Naked, Marco Marsan, Jodere Group, 2003.

The Art of Possibility, Rosamund Stone Zander & Benjamin Zander, Harvard Business School Press, 2000.

The Artist's Way, Julia Cameron, Jeremy P. Tarcher/Putnam, 1992, 2002.

How to Think like Leonardo da Vinci, Michael J. Gelb, Bantam Dell, 2004.

The Playful Way to Knowing Yourself, Roberta Allen, Houghton Mifflin Company, 2003.

Your personal reading list

Make a list of books you think will help in your
Warrior and Little Girl Journey.

_____

_____

_____

_____

_____

_____

_____

_____

_____

_____

About the Author

Geri Rhoades is President of Renewed Direction, a communication coaching and consulting practice. She has an MBA and a Master of Arts in Communication. As an executive for national and international companies and as a CEO coach and communication/change management trainer, Geri Rhoades brings over 20 years of diverse experience to her clients. She currently works with women in helping them discover the Warrior's power and the Little Girl that brings them joy. She can be contacted at www.reneweddirection.com for speaking and workshop engagements.

Quick Order Form

Fax orders: 781-237-4357. Send this form.
Telephone orders: Call 781-237-4357.
email orders: orders@Tanzanitepress.com
Postal orders: Tanzanite Press; P.O. Box 620674, Newton Lower Falls, MA 02462-0674

Please send the following copies of The Warrior and The Little Girl.

Quantity:_____

☐ Please send me information on speaking engagements and consulting.

Name:_____

Address:_____

City:_____ State:_____ Zip_____

Telephone:_____

email address:_____

Payment: ☐ Credit Card: ☐ Check
        ☐ Visa   ☐ Mastercard   ☐ AMEX

Card number:_____

Name on Card: _____ Exp. date_____

Sales tax: Please add 5% for products shipped to Massachusetts addresses.

Please inscribe my book to: _____